People of the Saltwater

PEOPLE OF THE SALTWATER

An Ethnography of Git lax m'oon

Charles R. Menzies

University of Nebraska Press · Lincoln and London

A portion of chapter 5 originally appeared as a part of a longer essay, "The Indigenous Foundation of the Resource Economy of BC's North Coast," *Labour/Le Travail* 61 (Spring): 131–49. An earlier version of chapter 7 originally appeared as "Dm sibilhaa'nm da laxyuubm gitxaała: Picking abalone in gitxaała territory," *Human Organization* 69, no. 3 (2010). An earlier version of chapter 8 appeared as "The Disturbed Environment: The Indigenous Cultivation of Salmon," in *Keystone Nations: Indigenous Peoples and Salmon across the North Pacific*, edited by Benedict Colombi and James Brooks, 161–82 (Santa Fe NM: School for Advanced Research).

All photographs in this volume are courtesy of the author.

Library of Congress Cataloging-in-Publication Data
Names: Menzies, Charles R., author.
Title: People of the saltwater: an ethnography of git lax m'oon / Charles R. Menzies.
Other titles: People of the saltwater, an ethnography of Gitxaala | Ethnography of git lax m'oon
Description: Lincoln: University of Nebraska Press, [2016] | Includes bibliographical references and index.
Identifiers: LCCN 2016010580
ISBN 9780803288089 (cloth: alk. paper)
ISBN 9780803291706 (pdf)
Subjects: LCSH: Tsimshian Indians—British Columbia—Prince Rupert Forest Region. | Tsimshian Indians—History. | Traditional fishing—British Columbia. | Tsimshian Indians—Politics and government.
Classification: LCC E99.T8 .M45 2016
| DDC 971.1004/974128—dc23
LC record available at http://lccn.loc.gov/2016010580

Set in Charis by Rachel Gould.

To the memory of Elizabeth Menzies *née* Gamble and Annette Dell *née* Gamble: Tsimshian matriarchs whose lives made an impact.

Contents

Illustrations

People of the Saltwater

Introduction

Git lax m'oon—people of the saltwater—that's who we are. We live on the
edge, in the extreme. We are the people of the saltwater. That's who we are.

ELMER MOODY, 2008

Git lax m'oon, people of the saltwater, also known as Gitxaała, are an
ancient Indigenous people of the northwestern coast of North America. The oral history of Gitxaała reach back to the time when ice covered the landscape and strange beings lived alongside humans. From
that time until the present Gitxaała have lived within our *laxyuup* (territory) without interruption. We have welcomed newcomers, repulsed
invaders, and enjoyed the beautiful place that is our home.

Contemporary Lach Klan, the home village of Gitxaała, has been
continuously occupied for millennia, over ten thousand years according to oral tradition, at least five thousand according to science. In the
past there were many other Gitxaała villages throughout our laxyuup.
However, the effects of colonialism, a significant population collapse
caused by the spread of foreign diseases brought by late eighteenth-
century European travelers, led us to gather our people together at
Lach Klan. Throughout our history Lach Klan has retained a special
significance as a culturally important gathering place, even while
Gitxaała lived spread throughout the laxyuup in many other villages.

This book tells one part of Gitxaała's story. I make no claims to a definitive account. My telling is steeped in my own memories and experiences and rooted in interviews, conversations, and discussions with
other Gitxaała people. I also draw upon a rich archival record that

1

documents the more recent story of Gitxaała over the past two centuries. Ultimately this is my account of Gitxaała. Nonetheless it is also an account that has been shaped by my family, friends, and colleagues. No matter how individual a particular work is in its writing and conception, what we produce as humans is ultimately a social product that rests upon the goodwill, knowledge, and support of others.

While Gitxaała and this place have always been a part of my history and who I am, the formal research upon which this book is based began in the late 1990s. I have always been intrigued by the development of extractive resource industries such as fisheries and forestry. This interest manifested in a series of projects documenting First Nations' involvement in forestry (Menzies and Butler 2001). As research progressed, the focus shifted from a regional pan-Tsimshian perspective to a specific Gitxaała-based program. In 2001 a formal protocol was adopted in a letter of intent from me and public affirmation from Gitxaała through a series of luncheons and dinners (Menzies 2004). The luncheons and dinners (hosted by me) are critical acts of acknowledging community direction and input, taking advice, and returning information and research products to community. While mail and electronic transfers of data might technically return information to community, it is only with the publicly witnessed act that one can say, within a Gitxaała perspective, that one has done what one set out to do and has fulfilled one's intention to carry out respectful research. The protocol essentially licensed my use of information gathered through community-supported research and affirmed Gitxaała's sovereign rights over their own intellectual property. This is a living process constantly reaffirmed, renegotiated, and enacted through a lifelong process of public witnessing.

My late mother, Shirley Marie Menzies (née Naud), inspired in me a thirst for stories about family and lives well lived. Though she was not from Gitxaała, it was through her that I leaned to honor and value my family and my family's history. My great-aunt Annette (Nettie) Dell (née Gamble) would talk about her father, Sm'ooygit Tsibassa (Edward Gamble). Later my father would tell me more about the life of this man. These three people—my mother, my aunt, and my father—shared their memories with me in a way that has inspired my own search for greater understanding of the history and place that I am from, laxyuup Gitxaała on British Columbia's north coast.

Marvin (Teddy) Gamble has been a like a brother and an uncle. Over nearly two decades we drank gallons of coffee together as we talked and joked. Our conversations have ranged from the mundane matters of daily life to shared enthusiasm about our own family's history. Later in this book I discuss more explicitly some of our shared experiences and travels through laxyuup Gitxaała; for now I simply mention the importance of friendship and family relations.

This journey has also been shaped by my cousin Merle Bolton (Teddy's sister) and her husband, Ernie Bolton. Each in their own way has played an important role in this story. Merle has hosted me, and countless students, in her home over the years. Her advice and direction have helped to clarify my perspective of my Gitxaała home. Ernie has been a research associate and an uncle. We have worked together, gone fishing once or twice, and had a lot of fun smoking fish in his sister Alberta's smokehouse. Caroline Butler has been part of this research, first as a student and now as an accomplished researcher in her own right. Together Caroline, Ernie, and I have worked through many theoretical and methodological matters that underlie the account that follows. These friendships and family relations give strength and depth to my reflections on the world of Gitxaała. All of these people have, in their own way, welcomed me home.

Arriving Home

The DeHavilland Beaver banks hard over. The pilot examines the water below us before landing the small plane. I get my final aerial view of Lach Klan, the village that many of my relatives live in, as the plane touches down. Thirty miles to the southwest of Prince Rupert on British Columbia's north coast, visitors could be forgiven for thinking this is a remote and isolated place.

This is the first time that I have actually visited the village. Even though I grew up on the north coast and spent much of my time on the water working with my father on his commercial seine boat, I've never actually stepped ashore here. I have fished in the waters around Lach Klan, but my knowledge of the village is what my family have told me. As I looked down from the floatplane I tried to imagine the place as I had heard about it growing up: wooden boardwalks along the shore, large plank houses, memorial poles, my grandfather's store. But from my vantage point in the air the village looks like almost any other small coastal village: rows of houses, a cluster of what seem like administrative buildings, and a small dock crowded with fishing boats and small skiffs.

The purpose of this trip was to meet with the elected Band Council and ask for their collaboration in a research project I was planning. Ultimately more important to me, and to the subsequent work that I have been doing with and on behalf of Gitxaała, was the introduction to relatives, some of whom I had never met. The powerful thing about coming home to Lach Klan was that even if I didn't know who my people were, they certainly seemed to know who I was.

My father tells a story of his mother's funeral. He was twelve. He stood beside his father in the receiving line. "I didn't know I had so many relatives," he said. "They came up, spoke with my father, and then would take my hand. They all seemed to know me. I had no idea who they were."

The sense of being known even if one doesn't understand why or how is a powerful part of Indigenous society, where one's identity is defined by relations and family. Like my father before me, I found that my family in Lach Klan knew me.

Stepping from the plane onto the dock I wasn't sure quite what to do. Before I had much time to think a man named Vince Davis, whom I later came to know, asked me if I was heading up to the school. "Okay," he said. "Meet me at the van." Vince is one of a couple of informal taxi services in the village. He knew to expect me and made sure to get me to where I needed to go. From the moment he dropped me at the door of a relative's home the rest of my day was structured by a rapid-fire series of visits and introductions to family members. While I vaguely recall my meeting with the Band Council, I vividly remember each meeting with family, especially the amazing oolichan dinner held at Teddy Gamble's house for me.

From this first visit in 1998 a productive stream of collaborative research projects have developed, including the examination of First Nations involvement in forestry (Menzies and Butler 2001), selective fishing gear (Menzies and Butler 2007), and traditional ecological knowledge (Menzies 2006, 2010). This work has created opportunities for students, colleagues, and community members and has expanded to include archaeological research and documentary film production. Throughout, this work has been linked by an overarching concern with resource use, management, and harvesting. Out of all of this has emerged the current book, which locates Gitxaała in history, place, and practice.

When I started my research I didn't explicitly set out to do "Indigenous research," but then, neither did I set out to do "anthropology." I simply wanted to write about and explore the place where I am from. Given the politics of research, one is compelled to be clear, to make choices, or be pushed off the fence. I am not known to sit on fences. That said, I have at times tried to balance incommensurate perspectives when balance was not really feasible.

In the summer of 1990 media coverage of the Oka Crisis, a rights battle between members of the Mohawk community of Kanesatake and the Quebec town of Oka that erupted into an armed confrontation, washed across Canada. In Prince Rupert white fishermen and their allies rallied against aboriginal rights and title, and the Tsimshian Nation and its allies demonstrated in support of the Mohawk and for First Nations rights and title. As an aspiring researcher I eagerly attended all of the rallies and protests.

I grew up in Prince Rupert. I knew, worked and went to school with, and was related to people involved in the white anti-Indian protests and the Tsimshian pro–aboriginal rights demonstrations. I learned of the different events from networks of family and friends. At both events I spoke with people I knew, listened to concerns, and took notes and photos. For a neophyte researcher it was exciting: I felt in the middle of things as I worked to record a balanced view.

On my way home from our boat a day or two after the protest and demonstration I met a fisherman I had known for years.

"Hey," he said. I stopped to talk. We were standing by a rail line behind the now defunct and demolished Prince Rupert Fishermen's Co-op.

"I hear what you've been doing," he said.

"What do you mean?"

"You were marching with those Indians."

"I was also at the blockade in the morning. You saw me there."

"There is only one side." He raised his hand above my face, his fingers held in the shape of a gun. He cocked the "gun" and touched the muzzle to my forehead—BANG. Silenced, I watched him turn and walk away. (See Menzies 1994 for a more detailed discussion of these events and issues.)

In the face of the colonial expropriation of Indigenous peoples and the associated social and physical violence enacted upon us there can be only one reasonable outcome, only one reasonable approach to research: to take on, as one takes on a name, the weight and responsibility of an Indigenous approach to decolonization (Coulthard 2014; Fanon 1963). The context in which my research takes place means that my work is definitionally situated within that body of work inspired by a decolonial methodology (Smith 1999) and rooted in an Indigenous perspective. There is no fence to sit on here. Who I am shapes what I do. Memories of family events—traumatic and joyous, our legacies of colonialism— adhere to our sensibilities and result in sets of behaviors and decisions that contribute to a way of engaging with relations and strangers; it's what I refer to as forming the basis to a method of respectful research.

My doctoral research in France was freeing in that I had been presented with what was essentially a blank slate, no history to either link or ensnare me. Yet it was shallow and missed nuances that could come to light only with years of experience or the intimacy of belonging. The power of intimacy—in the sense of careful, close, empathetic, and detailed comprehension—is that one becomes part of the story one is writing. This is my approach to anthropological research.

I draw inspiration from Kevin Dwyer's (1982) sense of anthropology as dialogue, a conversation between people in which we all learn. I have also found Max Gluckman's (1958) analysis of social situations instructive; with observations, conversations, and detailed background knowledge, he was able to parse out the dynamics of social and racial relations in 1930s southern Africa from a series of social situations orbiting the opening of a new bridge. These are not specifically Indigenous research methods (if such a thing can truly be said to exist).[1] They are, however, good tools that facilitate understanding and analysis.

Indigenous methodology, as articulated in a growing field of publications, purports to represent something new. I am not convinced. The strength of books like *Decolonizing Methodologies* is that Linda Smith (1999) calls out the fundamental problem of the imbalance of power and control over and within the research process. Echoing her critique, hereditary leaders from Gitxaała constantly remind Canada and British Columbia that the authority and jurisdiction to make decisions related to Gitxaała territory rests with the chiefs, not the crown. If there is an Indigenous methodology, it is rooted in decolonizing contemporary power structures of the state. It will require non-Indigenous researchers stepping back, turning their gaze, and following rather than directing (Menzies 2011).

Organization of the Book

This book is divided into two main parts. In the first I outline the social and political relations that constitute Gitxaała society and lay the foundation of being Gitxaała. The second part focuses on the enactment of cultural practices through Gitxaała fisheries.

Social and political relations within Gitxaała society are governed by key social institutions of political leadership (social organization), territory, and history. I explore in detail each of these key social institutions. Each chapter seeks to identify the underlying traditional forms of these institutions and to also explore the ways they have changed and persisted through the disruption of colonialism and the rise of an industrial capitalist economy. Chapter 1 situates the story of Gitxaała within the wider Tsimshianic world and the importance of naming our Indigenous community with our own terms.

Taking inspiration from the title of the hereditary leadership, *smgigyet*—real people—chapter 2 outlines the traditional organization of Gitxaała society. In this chapter, however, I am not concerned simply with attempting to reconstruct an abstract model of what may have been. Rather the chapter opens with a description of social organization and then explores the points of continuity and change as Gitxaała people navigated the disruptions of the colonial period and the development of industrial resource capitalism.

Political leadership and social organization are intimately linked to place, to the laxyuup (territory) of Gitxaała; for example, a chief's wealth lies within his laxyuup. Chapter 3 interrogates the ideas of territoriality: how it emerged, developed, and altered through time and how it applies to the place where Gitxaała people live. The traditional accounts of laxyuup are explored in the context of the formation of reserves created by the colonial government and more recent litigation between Gitxaała and Canada.

Chapter 4 outlines the ways Gitxaała historical knowledge is transmitted within and between generations. We are a people steeped in our *adaawx*, our history. Our society has persisted for millennia, but beyond that Gitxaała is a society in which linking the present with the past is of critical importance. Ideas of political leadership and territory, for example, are supported, taught, and reinforced through historical knowledge. Knowledge required for the proper management of the laxyuup (in both intangible and tangible ways) is passed intergenerationally through the medium of history.

The second part of the book turns from the nature of social institutions to ways that Gitxaała enact critical cultural values through the practice of fisheries. Fisheries and related natural resource harvesting form a critical core of the cultural practices of Gitxaała. These are also critical economic components of Gitxaała society. This part of the book begins with an overview of Gitxaała fisheries (chapter 5) and then examines Gitxaała fisheries in relation to three culturally important species: *tskah* and *xs'waanx* (herring and herring roe), *bilhaa* (abalone), and *hoon* (salmon). Each of the case studies examines a fishery that has ancient roots in Gitxaała history and an important contemporary place in Gitxaała's world.

Tskah and xs'waanx (chapter 6) provided a range of food resources (roe in several forms plus the flesh; fresh, dried, or smoked) historically and into the present day. Gitxaała's relationship with herring is an example of how the process of colonization has contributed to a narrowing of utilization. Bilhaa is a culturally important species; it is also a species that has been devastated by ill-conceived bio-economic management models. Chapter 7 examines the harvesting techniques that maintained sustainable harvest levels for millennia and the grief caused by the externally driven collapse of the fishery. Hoon (chapter 8) is the iconic species that most coastal Indigenous groups along the north Pacific shore are identified with in popular imagination. Understanding the nature and importance of hoon and associated Gitxaała harvesting practices tells us a great deal about the the relationship between human interventions in our environment and the health and well-being of hoon themselves. The capacity to maintain large harvests of hoon over millennia required a detailed and nuanced understanding of the ecology of Gitxaała's own laxyuup and the behavior of the hoon themselves.

The łagyigyet (old people) lived in a world of wonder and change at the beginning of time. Modern Gitxaała are also living in a world of wonder and change. This book is my account of the world brought into being by the łagyigyet through the eyes of Gitxaała today. I open my house to you, Reader. Come, sit down at the table, and take your place. I have a story to tell.

Git lax m'oon

Gitxaała and the Names Anthropologists Have Given Us

Gitxaała people live in a breathtakingly beautiful place on the north coast of British Columbia. We call ourselves the Git lax m'oon—the people of the saltwater—in recognition of where we have lived since time immemorial: on the islands and inlets of this rugged piece of coastline. Gitxaała people know this is a harsh place to live, but "we choose to live here," Chief Elmer Moody reminded people at a feast in 2008 to affirm and recognize Gitxaała territory in the presence of federal and provincial government representatives. This coastline is the place Gitxaała people call home.

This book tells the story of Gitxaała, an ancient people living on the saltwater. It is also a story being told from the perspective of someone who is both a professional stranger (Agar 1996) and a community member. I have grown up hearing about and living in this place. As a professional stranger, that is, a practicing anthropologist, I have conducted anthropological research on the north coast of British Columbia since 1988 and with the Gitxaała Nation since 1998. My research has been focused on the political economy of Indigenous societies and the subsequent transition to an industrial capitalist economy based on natural resources extraction (Menzies and Butler 2008). As part of this research I have explored the relations between aboriginal and nonaboriginal people (Menzies 1994, 1996) and written about Indigenous ecological knowledge (Menzies 2010, 2012; Menzies and Butler 2007). I have also written about nonaboriginal communities in the commercial fishing industry (Menzies 1993). My love for and abiding interest in this place arises out of my family's personal connection to it. Elsewhere (Menzies 1994) I explore in more detail my personal and familial ties to this place. In the pages that follow I at times make reference to my place in this work, but my focus is on the social and productive world of Gitxaała, and thus my personal story is of note only insofar as is it gives passion and direction to my inquiries, reflections, and commentary. Thus, while in this book I draw upon all of my prior experience, my focus is on Gitxaała, the people and our place in the world.

Gitxaała's main village today, Lach Klan, is located on the edge of Hecate Strait, about thirty miles to the southwest of the town of Prince Rupert. The traditional territory, or laxyuup, of Gitxaała (see chapter 3) extends from about Prince Rupert south 150 miles to Aristazabal Island, taking in most of the coastal islands and the adjoining mainland. This is a rugged marine and terrestrial space. However, one should be cautious in thinking it to be an isolated or pristine space.

Notions of isolation and remoteness are relative and situational. For an urban-based audience the tales and descriptions of the Gitxaała world may well elicit a strong sense of the pristine wilderness or may even evoke a sense of danger or foreboding. It is indeed a hard place to get to and to travel through if one does not own or have access to a boat. Difficulty of access, however, does not make a place remote. It is the lack of familiarity with the place that gives the laxyuup Gitxaała an aura of isolation to those not from this area. A sense of familiarity can also mask real material conditions of isolation and disconnection from a wider social and economic world. Thus even as Gitxaała people remain intimately familiar with our territory and home it is possible that as the wider world globalizes, our connection to place may restrict and then marginalize our capacity to continue living where and how we want to. This is nonetheless the place within which Gitxaała people have lived for millennia. Life is lived out here. Oral histories relate to events and places here. Throughout the laxyuup one can find material evidence of Gitxaała use and history: ancient villages, stone structures built for fishing and the cultivation of bivalves in creeks and along the foreshore, and contemporary camps, cabins, and anchorages.

This is not a strange or pristine place waiting to be found or discovered. This is in fact the mundane everyday world through which Gitxaała people travel as we return generation after generation to fishing camps, hunting grounds, seaweed-picking spots, and fishing grounds far from shore. This is a place within which people are living, shaping, and using on an everyday basis. While this may be a place removed from the centers of today's metropolitan world, for Gitxaała people this is home.

This book, in telling Gitxaała's story, aims to bring forward our world, a world that to us is familiar and friendly (though it is not without peril and dangers). I discuss how Gitxaała society is organized, the nature and extent of Gitxaała territory, and how knowledge is passed along from one generation to the next. I explain how Gitxaała people have made their livelihood from the bounty of the laxyuup historically and into the present. While this world may remain remote to your daily life, I trust that it will have become more familiar and understandable by the end.

Gitxaała people have lived on this coast at least since the last ice age ten thousand years ago. The oral history of Gitxaała contains traces of the ancient past, when large islands existed to the west in the middle of today's Hecate Strait. Other histories tell of a time and place covered in snow and ice. Still other histories document the arrival and emergence within Gitxaała territory of prominent chiefs and families.

Archaeological research that I have conducted reveals continuously inhabited villages dating back many millennia. Stone tools and debris from making these tools found along the foreshore in the southern reaches of Gitxaała territory have been dated through comparison with similar stone tool collections to at least six thousand years ago. Archaeologists working in adjoining territories have found evidence of human occupation going back at least as long as the timeline within Gitxaała territory (Mackie et al. 2011; Martindale et al. 2009; McLaren et al. 2011). This is an ancient place and these are an ancient people whose traditions and society continue into the present.

What's in a Name?

According to anthropologists and linguists, Gitxaała are a Tsimshianic people. Academic researchers have historically used language as a key attribute to classify different peoples. Since Gitxaała shares a common language family, culture, and history with the Nisga'a (who live along the Nass River) and the Gitxsan (who live along the interior reaches of the Skeena River and its tributaries), Gitxaała has been grouped within the wider ethnographical category of Tsimshian. Gitxaała people, however, have always understood ourselves to be a unique people resident on the outer coastal islands, people of the saltwater, people out to sea. We recognize a common connection with our cousins to the north, east, and south, but Gitxaała are the original inhabitants of the coast and thus see ourselves as a different people.

Gitxaała is a matrilineal society; that is, family group membership and descent is reckoned through one's mother. Yet a traditional system of arranged marriage ensured that inheritance of key resources such as hereditary names and associated property actually passed along patrilineal lines from grandfather to grandson. This raises interesting questions about the emergence of patrilineal inheritance in the mid-twentieth century. Given the ancient practice of combining patrilineality with matrilineality, it is likely that what started to occur in terms of the shift to patrilineal inheritance in the early twentieth century was actually rooted in the earlier system, which conserved lineage property through an alternation of ownership between corporate groups from one generation to the next. It may well be that ideas of patrilineality in descent coexisted with ideas of matrilineality in corporate group membership well before Christian missionaries began to attack matrilineal kin groups within the Tsimshianic world.

The coastal Tsimshianic world includes several separate village-based communities, of which Gitxaała is one. Gitxaała people understand our place on the coast quite differently than did early academic commentators or our more acculturated Indigenous cousins who live in Port Simpson, for example. Gitxaała people proudly proclaim that we have remained in our central village, Lach Klan, without interruption for millennia, while other coastal Tsimshianic villages deserted their territories in the face of expanding industrial resource extraction capitalism. Gitxaała people, however, found a way to hold on to tradition and participate in the capitalist economy.

Throughout this book I refer to the people now living in Lax Kw'alaams (Port Simpson) and Metlakatla as Coast Tsimshian. This is a reference to their genesis as a discrete Indigenous people following contact, when they regrouped around the communities formed by the Hudson Bay Company trading post and the Christian missionary William Duncan. Ts'msyen is a term used to refer to those people who identify themselves as living in connection to the Skeena River. Unless otherwise noted, I refer to the people who are part of the Gitxaała Nation as Gitxaała. I also make occasional reference to Tsimshianic peoples, which is a broad anthropological designation that includes the Nisga'a and the Gitxsan within the other coastal and in-river Tsimshianic peoples.

No terms are ever fixed firmly in time, nor are such terms immune to the vicissitudes of political machinations. In recent years, partly in response to ongoing litigation between Gitxaała and other Tsimshian groups and between Gitxaała and the Canadian state, the terms Coast Tsimshian and Southern Tsimshian have become codified in a way that deviates from much earlier anthropological work, in which the primary distinction highlighted was linguistic. The evolution of these terms has also shifted away from a more ecological-political sense deployed by Marsden (2002).

The early twentieth-century references to Coast Tsimshian essentially include all of the Tsimshianic peoples from the Kitselas Canyon on the Skeena River near the contemporary town of Terrace out to the coast, including the communities of Port Simpson, Metlakatla, Kitkatla, Hartley Bay, and Klemtu (where some of the descendents of the former Kitasoo Tsimshian community now reside).

The original anthropological terms for Tsimshianic peoples were rooted in a linguistic and sociocultural system of categorization used by early twentieth-century anthropologists. Three basic Tsimshianic languages were identified: Nisga'a, Gitxsan, and Coast Tsimshian. This linguistic approach allowed anthropologists to systematically compare the various Indigenous peoples they encountered. Language was understood to be closely tied to cultural traits, and together they provided the backbone to a grand anthropological classificatory scheme of Indigenous North Americans. However, this approach to labeling Indigenous societies and peoples tended to ignore the ways local communities self-identified.

The idea that there had been a fourth Tsimshianic language emerged following John Dunn's (1969, 1976) linguistic research with fluent Coast

Tsimshian speakers in Lach Klan (Gitxaała's primary nineteenth- and twentieth-century village), Prince Rupert, and Hartley Bay in the late 1960s and early 1970s. Drawing upon his research in Gitxaała and with speakers from Hartley Bay and Klemtu, Dunn suggested that there used to be an older language, now essentially extinct, called Southern Tsimshian (Halpin and Seguin 1990; Miller 1984; Seguin 1984). For Dunn this was a linguistic designation. However, by the time Halpin and Seguin (1990) published their overview essay on the Tsimshian in the *Handbook of North American Indians* they were distinguishing between Coast and Southern Tsimshian to unproblematically demarcate sociopolitical and historical differences within the peoples formally labeled Coast Tsimshian by anthropologists. It is worthwhile to explore the history of Southern Tsimshian as an anthropological label in a bit more detail as it encapsulates some of the serious difficulties inherent in social science classifications of Indigenous peoples.

In his ethnography, *Tsimshian Culture: A Light through the Ages*, Jay Miller (1997, 16) says this about the term Southern Tsimshian: "Until a few years ago, the existence of another language on the coast, now called Southern Tsimshian, went unrecognized. It was spoken in three or so villages on the islands and inlets south of the mouth of the Skeena." Earlier Miller (1984, 31) was more circumspect about the geographical extent of the Southern Tsimshian:

> The Southern Tsimshian consist of the villages of Klemtu, Hartley Bay, and perhaps Kitkatla at an even earlier period. The major criterion for establishing this grouping is the use of a hitherto unrecognized language, sgüümk, sküüxs, still used by a handful of speakers in Klemtu and Hartley Bay. Hartley Bay used the language before members joined Duncan at Old Metlakatla for a short time and switched to the coast language. It is not yet certain that sküüxs was used in Kitkatla in the past, but the history of intermarriage and feasting among these villages strongly suggests that Kitkatla should be included in the group.

Dunn (1969, 1976), the linguist whose work gave rise to the term Southern Tsimshian, is clear in his initial account that his subject is a linguistic, not a sociopolitical designation. However, like Halpin, Seguin, and others in the small cohort then studying coastal Tsimshianic peoples, Miller came to use the term in a broader ethnographic fashion as he sought to understand and describe ethnographically observable differences within and between the various coastal Tsimshianic communities.

Coastal Tsimshianic peoples did in fact have different experiences of interaction following initial contact with Europeans. Village groups based in the lower Skeena River consolidated around the Hudson Bay trading post staring in the 1830s (Marsden and Galois 1995). Marsden (2002) argues that the Coastal Tsimshian (she prefers the term Northern Tsimshian) were already an integrated regional alliance prior to contact with Europeans and prior to regrouping at the Hudson Bay fort. However, the evidence for Marsden's conclusion is not definitive. What is clear is that through the fur trading and early commercial fishing period what was once an ecological-political integration became a clear residential and political amalgamation in Port Simpson and then a bit later in Metlakatla. Later still in the nineteenth century the entire community of Hartley Bay pulled up stakes and relocated to the mission town of Metlakatla near Prince Rupert. Then, toward the end of the century, the Tsimshianic peoples living at the southern extent of the region around Kitasoo Bay and Higgins Pass deserted their villages and regrouped with Xaisxais people to the south in the cannery town of Klemtu (Miller 1981). Only the Gitxaała people stayed in their primary village site of Lach Klan—though not without suffering the depredation of the diseases that plagued nineteenth-century coastal aboriginal communities (Boyd 1999).

Many of the late twentieth-century ethnographers and researchers who came to this changed social landscape looked for ways to distinguish their particular communities of study from others and to reflect the historical factors that resulted in a reduction to five coastal Tsimshian villages from more than fourteen only a century and a half previously. The five resulting villages are, from south to north, Klemtu, Hartley Bay, Lach Klan, Metlakatla, and Port Simpson. Here we see the central heuristic importance of Marsden's (2002, 101–2) tripartite model of Northern, Southern, and Interior Tsimshian. Marsden's model draws from the internal histories of the people themselves and then locates spheres of social and economic interaction and alliance within functional ecological units such as unique watersheds. The tripartite model tells us more about the historical attributes of interaction than does the more politicized Coast/Southern model that emerged out of struggles in the court system and contemporary political pronouncements by today's Coast Tsimshian leadership.

Not all ethnographers of the Tsimshianic peoples were focused on highlighting internal differences. James McDonald (1984; writing in the same volume as Miller 1984) uses the term Tsimshian to survey the rich economic pattern of Tsimshianic involvement in the emerging nineteenth-century capitalist economy. McDonald's point is that rather than "having been shunted off from the main track into reserves [the Tsimshian] were often critical to the success of various industries" (40; see also Menzies and Butler 2008). He refers to individual Tsimshian from a range of villages later labeled Coast (Port Simpson and Metlakatla) and Southern (Lach Klan, Hartley Bay, and Klemtu) by Miller, Seguin, Halpin, et al. McDonald's point, I would argue, is that the fundamental issue is not that of a reconstructed past but an examination of how Indigenous actors intervened in, accommodated, and resisted the rise of industrial resource extraction capitalism. In this context, using labels that highlighted internal ethnic differences would have obscured the common processes acting upon these communities.

Both theoretical approaches—the political-economic followed by McDonald and the structuralist-reconstructivist followed by Seguin, Halpin, and Miller—have their roots in theories and philosophies established outside of Indigenous communities. While these approaches do have value and have contributed to our understanding of the world of the Tsimshianic peoples, they often overshadow community-based explanations and priorities. The way the term Southern Tsimshian has emerged, first as a linguistic marker and then as a sociopolitical label, is a case in point. In the context of recent research the unproblematic adoption of this term has had profound real-time consequences for the Indigenous peoples on the north coast. This book presents an Indigenous counterpoint rooted in Gitxaała history and practice.

Most research into Tsimshianic communities has been on reconstructions of culture, belief, and traditional practices, to the exclusion of involvement in the contemporary economy. This has been driven, to a certain extent, by litigation in which the legal profession and judicial system ask for proof of cultural practices having existed prior to, at the time of, and beyond the point of contact with Europeans. But it still reflects the dominating interest of non-Indigenous researchers seeking cultural laboratories to test their theories and models.

Returning to the emergence of the terms Coast and Southern Tsimshian, a consultant, Joan Lovisek, working on behalf of the Canadian government in the case of the fishing rights and title of Allied Tsimshian Tribes (most of whom now live in Port Simpson and Metlakatla), picked up the terms Coast Tsimshian and Southern Tsimshian in her attempt to critique their claim of an aboriginal right to fish commercially. Drawing upon an early twentieth-century model of acculturation Lovisek suggested that contemporary peoples living in Port Simpson and Metlakatla had a tenuous connection with the aboriginal customs and practices of the people who had proceeded them and who had once lived in Prince Rupert Harbor and adjoining areas. Drawing extensively upon the postmodernist archaeological writings of Andrew Martindale (though misinterpreting his conclusions in several critical ways), Lovisek constructed a Coastal Tsimshian society that emerged in the aftermath of the dislocation and disruption caused by contact with the European-based economy. Critically Lovisek located the origins of the Coast Tsimshian in the proto-contact period, but not coming fully into its own until well after the establishment of a new capitalist economy in the mid- to late nineteenth century. Her argument is not totally wrong; she does carefully detail how the colonial period disrupted the Ts'msyen living at the mouth of the Skeena and how this disruption transformed them into the Coast Tsimshian. However, she overstates her case in terms of the nature of the discontinuity, and because she misreads Martindale she misunderstands the extent of the continuity between the earlier Ts'msyen and the contemporary Coast Tsimshian.[1]

Subsequently, in the context of inter-Tsimshianic ligation, consultants working on behalf of Metlakatla and Lax Kw'alaams (including but not restricted to George MacDonald, Joanne MacDonald, and Richard Inglis)[2] also used the terms to highlight their interpretation of Coast Tsimshian rights and title in opposition to any potential overlapping rights and title claims advanced by Gitxaała. Here we can see the life history of the term Southern Tsimshian starting to take on a rather pernicious quality. Far from being merely a linguistic designation or an ecological-political descriptor, the terms have now risen to the status of ethnic designations in which the frontier between Coast and Southern Tsimshian is expressed as a fixed and impermeable boundary. As we will see, such a firmly fixed designation, while reflecting a grain of truth, is ultimately complicit with a colonial act of appropriation and disposition enacted by renaming a people with an externally imposed name.

There are of course clear historical, social, and cultural distinctions that have emerged over the long course of time. The recent designation of Coast versus Southern Tsimshian, however, is tied to conflicts and struggles over control and access to scarce economic resources, complicated by the intervention of a neoliberal state intent on limiting aboriginal rights and title as much as possible. For governments and their associated business partners the stakes are very high. Being able to suppress aboriginal rights and title works to the advantage of these corporate agents. Having complicit First Nations to partner with and to act as proxies in conflicts with other First Nations allows a sort of red-washing, whereby governments and corporations can proclaim aboriginal-friendly projects while simultaneously restraining aboriginal rights. It is in this particular context that the recent designations of Coast Tsimshian and Southern Tsimshian has emerged. With this in mind I nonetheless refer to the people now living in Port Simpson (also known as Lax Kw'alaams) and Metlakatla as Coast Tsimshian (since this is the term they are actively deploying today) and call the other communities by their village name (Gitxaała, Gitga'ata [Hartley Bay], Kitasoo [Klemtu], Kitsumkalum, and Kitselas). As I noted, I use the term Tsimshianic when speaking of the wider ethnographic community, which includes the Nisga'a and Gitxsan. When speaking of the traditional precontact lives of the Coast Tsimshian I use the term Ts'msyen (people of the Skeena River).

Writing Gitxaała

There is a dearth of academic research that specifically addresses Gitxaała as a subject of study separate from other Tsimshianic communities. There are published academic and archival academic materials that make reference to Gitxaała in the context of the wider Tsimshianic world (Marsden 2002; Miller 1997; Roth 2008). There are historical records, such as ships' logs and government documents, that make specific reference to Gitxaała (for example, James Colnett in 1787 [published in Galois 2004]; J. Caamano in 1792 [Wagner and Newcombe 1938]; Charles Bishop in 1795 [Roe 1967]). There is a living oral tradition in Gitxaała that maintains an active account of the past. While suffering the depredations of colonialism, like other Indigenous peoples in the Americas, Gitxaała has nonetheless maintained continuous habitation and use within their core territories.

The anthropological literature is replete with descriptions of Gitxaała as the most conservative of the Tsimshianic groups. Inglis et al. (1990, 288) comment, "At Port Simpson and Metlakatla, Kitkatla has the reputation of being the 'most Indian' of the Tsimshian villages, which concurs with the assessment given by Dorsey (1897, 280)." William Beynon, a Coast Tsimshian who worked as an ethnographer with Franz Boas and Marius Barbeau (among others), writes in his 1916 field notes that the Gitxaała people "have not advanced as much as the other people, of other tribes in matters of education and still adhere to ancient ceremonies."[3] Beynon was not being complimentary—he was in fact complaining that this adherence to ancient ceremonies was restricting his ethnographic research—but his point highlights how Gitxaała have endeavored to retain the old ways in the face of their neighbors' adaptation to and taking on of Euro-Canadian ways. Gitxaała's cultural conservatism can also be seen in the census of 1891, in which the names of the people in Metlakatla are nearly 100 percent Anglo and in Fort Simpson (later changed to Port Simpson) are mostly Anglo, while in Gitxaała the names are nearly 100 percent sm'algyax (Tsimshianic language). The continuing conservatism is reflected in the relatively small number of researchers who have been able to work successfully in and with Gitxaała over the twentieth century.

Beynon recorded details of contemporary hunting territories, the oral history that explains ownership of these territories, records of feasts and meetings that he directly observed (as well as those for which he recorded oral histories), comments on changes in ownership patterns, and the history of Indigenous fisheries. And this is only a partial list. Beynon was particularly interested in succession and inheritance of names. He himself used this knowledge to advance and secure his own hereditary rank and made many comments in his field notes on the range of practices and debates related to the taking on of hereditary names. Thus the early ethnographic literature is based on a very contemporary set of observations made by an ethnographer who was both a member and an observer of Coast Tsimshian society.

Most, if not all, of the early and mid-twentieth-century ethnographers of the Tsimshian world either worked directly with Beynon or used his massive collection of field notes, manuscripts, and commentaries. Celebrated early twentieth-century ethnographers Marius Barbeau, Franz Boas, Phillip Drucker, Homer Barnett, Viola Garfield, and Amelia Sussman all worked directly with Beynon and based much (if not all) of their subsequent Tsimshian-related published work on his research.[4] Beynon acted as both key informant (for example, with Garfield and Sussman) and lead researcher (for example, with Barbeau and Boas). Garfield (1939), a student of Boas, relied heavily on Beynon's research for her *Tsimshian Clan and Society*.

Subsequent ethnographers, such as Margaret Anderson (Seguin), John Cove, Marjorie Halpin, Susan Marsden, Jay Miller, James McDonald, and Christopher Roth drew extensively on Beynon's unpublished notes.[5] Of these late twentieth-century ethnographers, McDonald stands out as one of the first to engage in research with contemporary Tsimshianic people on topics of contemporary relevance, whereas most of the others relied almost exclusively on Beynon's work to study the Tsimshianic world or to structure their interviews of elders and hereditary leaders.

Archaeologists who have ventured into reviews and comments on oral history have also restricted themselves to consideration of previously published materials that are derivative of Beynon or have drawn directly from Beynon's unpublished notes. For example, while Kenneth Ames, Gary Coupland, Richard Inglis, Andrew Martindale, George MacDonald, and Paul Prince have written about or drawn inspiration from oral history, they have done so by direct reference to secondary literature or the unpublished notes of Beynon and have not engaged in systematic research on oral history with Tsimshianic people themselves. Thus these archaeologists reproduce what is essentially a vision of the Tsimshianic world inspired and structured by Beynon's intellectual work, in particular his unpublished 1950s multivolume work, "Ethnical and Geographical Study of the Tsimshian Nation."[6]

In one of the few published works to attempt an evaluation of the extent of Beynon's corpus, Barbara Winter (1984) highlights the ceremonial and mythic aspects of his work over the more contemporary or economic. However, Winter's analysis of Beynon's field notes was restricted to those

> texts recorded between 1937 and 1959, for Boas. These texts were selected for statistical testing because they represent a total sample of Beynon's work from a known period of time. A complete sample from a known period is not possible for the books sent to Barbeau as Barbeau removed the pages from the books and cut them into sections, each filed by subject. In the Boas collection are 256 narratives collected from 72 informants, as well as eyewitness accounts written from Beynon's personal experience. Beynon used three primary informants from whom he collected more than ten narratives, and a larger number from whom he elicited only one or two narratives. He relied on three informants to provide him with nearly twenty-five per cent of his data. These were Mark Luther (age 77, status not given), Joseph Bradley (age 90, chief), and Ethel Musgrave (elderly, chief). Of the twenty-four informants who provided him with nearly ninety per cent of his data, seven were chiefs, and between seven and eleven were councilors. Eighty-three per cent of his informants were men, and all of his female informants were of high status and/or elderly. (284)

Winter's analysis thus excludes all of the material that Beynon collected between 1915 and 1937 as well as the hundreds of pages of materials he collected in collaboration with Garfield, Sussman, Barbeau, Druckcr, and Barnett (to name only the most prominent scholars with whom Beynon worked during the period of Winter's analysis). Winter makes very clear the limitations of her analysis of Beynon's collected materials.

Wilson Duff, who utilized Beynon's materials in the 1960s as he prepared an expert report for the Nisga'a Nation, documents that Beynon did in fact record a fair bit of information that pertains to contemporary, economic, and territorial questions.[7] Having reviewed both Duff's notes and those prepared by Halpin from Duff's notes and hundreds of pages of notes collected directly by Beynon, I found that Beynon collected significant data that pertain directly to a wide range of topics, from traditional "salvage ethnography" to accounts of new types of aboriginal organizations such as the native Brotherhood of BC, of which he was an early member.

Beynon is the unsung hero of Tsimshianic research. Irrespective of his situated location within the Tsimshianic world, his work stands alone as a fundamentally important archive of knowledge. As I noted earlier, most anthropologists working in this region have relied extensively upon his work even though little of it has been published. In particular Beynon's "Ethnical and Geographical Study of the Tsimshian Nation" establishes what has become orthodoxy among Tsimshianic scholars: the stories of migration of the people now known as the Coast Tsimshian. (Beynon himself did not use that label, preferring to use the separate village or tribal names.)

McDonald extends and elaborates upon Beynon's work in a decisive fashion. Working primarily with Kitsumkalum, McDonald (1994) has focused on their involvement in wage labor, the economic relations in and basis of traditional Kitsumkalum society, and the ways these underlying forms have persisted and changed in the contemporary world. In his seminal article in the *American Ethnologist* McDonald (1994) documents the literal and figurative displacement of the Kitsumkalum from their own territory through the intersection of economic and legal processes. Drawing inspiration from dependency theory, he shows how the rise of the industrial economy transformed Kitsumkalum from being a central part of an integrated Indigenous regional economy to being set apart and marginalized from the industrial economy and their own territory.

John Pritchard's (1977) dissertation on the nearby Haisla is one of the few works that, like James A. McDonald's (1985), takes the role of aboriginal peoples in the contemporary economy seriously. In the 1970s anthropologists working along the northwest coast briefly flirted with political economy. This led them to ask questions about social class (see, for example, Kobrinsky 1975) and the rise of the industrial economy on the coast (Knight 1996; McDonald 1985; Pritchard 1977; Sewid and Spradley 1969). It is unfortunate, however, that the majority of researchers were more interested in reconstructing what had been than in understanding what was right in front of them.

There is scant mention of Gitxaała among scholars of Tsimshianic societies. Prior to the research of Caroline Butler and myself only a handful of people had conducted research directly with Gitxaała. John Dunn, a linguist, worked with Gitxaała people starting in the late 1960s. George and Joanne MacDonald (archaeologist and ethnographic curator, respectively) visited Lach Klan several times over the course of 1970s and 1980s.[8] Joanne MacDonald (2015) conducted a brief project on the Gitxaała stone masks (one of which is held by the Canadian Museum of History and the other by the Louvre). Dianne Newell (1999) spent five days onboard the Gitxaała fishing vessel *Western Spirit* in the early 1990s studying the roe-on-kelp fishery. McDonald has visited with and interviewed Gitxaała community members over the course of his three decades of northern BC research, though his primary focus has been Kitsumkalum, on the mid-reaches of the Skeena River.[9] More recently students working with Butler and me have conducted community research projects in Gitxaała (Menzies 2011; Menzies and Butler 2011).

The relative silence in the published literature makes writing about Gitxaała and Gitxaała's world important: there is something to say that has not been said publicly in writing. More than that, the silence on Gitxaała in the written record has created an opportunity for other voices to have a disproportionate weight in academic and legal debates. This book thus tells the story of Gitxaała from a perspective situated within the Gitxaała world. This is not, however, an authorized account, or what Noel Dyck (1993) has called an official ethnography. This is decidedly my perspective, my reading of the evidence and data that I have gathered over the course of my life and as a professional anthropologist. In some cases I will agree with colleagues writing from other places; in some cases I will disagree. But in all cases I will be clear about what the data I use and the various implications of the interpretations I make and how they are different from previous commentators'.

2

Smgigyet

Real People and Governance

Sm'ooygit, Sm'ooygit, Sm'ooygit He:l,
Smigigyet,
Lik'agyet,
Sigyidm hana'a,
K'abawaalksik

Thus do speeches and formal addresses in Gitxaała begin. These lines contain the key idea of Gitxaała governance as a system structured by social rank, connections to specific places through real people, and a profound historical sense that simultaneously looks to the past while asserting a living present and future.

Sm'ooygit means, literally, real (*sm*) people (*git*). The sm'ooygit (singular form) is the ranking hereditary leader. Other hereditary leaders of equivalent social standing form the *smgigyet* (plural form). In descending order of rank are the *lik'agyet* (councilors), *sigyidm hana'a* (matriarchs), and those women and men next in line to inherit chiefly names, *k'abawaalksik*.

In the invocation the leading sm'ooygit is directly acknowledged and addressed, affirming the hierarchical nature of Gitxaała society. Naming the leading sm'ooygit also locates Gitxaała geographically and temporally because hereditary names are tied to specific places and important events through lineage histories. Thus embedded in this simple greeting are the core principles of Gitxaała governance: rank and status, connections between place and person, and the presence of history and historical accounts in the actions of the present. Even in the face of massive changes in the surrounding world these principles of governance have been maintained and demonstrated by Gitxaała people time and time again, in formal feasts, weddings, community meetings, and public consultations with government and industry.

Gitxaała concerns with governance are a contemporary concern with ancient roots. Faced with growing demands from corporate developers, government agencies, and nonprofit organizations to meet and make decisions on social and economic development issues, Gitxaała's elected leadership organized a multiday community workshop and discussion on governance in 2008. Some leaders spoke on April 14:

> Gitxaała's claim. Who is responsible for advancing this claim? We need to strengthen what our position is going to be; our government structures; our governing structures. When we examine how to move forward we need to ask what are our roles, as Smgigyet, Sigyidm hana'a, Lik'agyet? What governance structures do we need? We need to develop a process for development, a governance structure so that our words don't just fall to the floor. (Elmer Moody, Laxgibu hereditary leader and chief councilor)[1]

> We can't do anything without Smgigyet. I want to support the speaker before me. We're happy to see smgigyet, hereditary leaders from Ganhada, Laskiik, Laxgibu. Happy what I've seen today. . . . We have a big issue coming up—self-government. We couldn't do it ourselves. We had to ask all you hereditary leaders to accomplish this. (Larry Bolton, Gispuwada hereditary leader)

> That's what my heart says—for what the previous speakers spoke. This is coming alive—what our old people did. I know this is going to be good for us. Sisters and brothers, keep it up, for keeping our village alive with the hereditary leaders. . . . Smgigyet, let us work together, we can do it. Whatever you have on your mind so that our village will run properly. My heart has been moved to see the people of Gitxaała are coming to do good for our village. Smgigyet of each clan, whatever you've got on your mind, don't

take it home, it is time to let it out so that our village will run properly. (Richard Spencer, Ganhada hereditary leader)

Communication is an important term. Our ancestors gathered together to communicate. Our laws are still here and in existence—always there for us. We need to revisit them and see where it would bring us. (Matthew Hill, Laskiik hereditary leader)

This is simultaneously culture in the making and culture in action. The structure, the pattern of speech is traditional—that is, in form and content—but it is also driven by a contemporary need to address governance issues here and now.

Other Indigenous nations, such as the Nisga'a, adopted a more Western-influenced system of governance that effectively set aside the authority and jurisdiction of the hereditary leadership. Gitxaała people have continuously rejected these accommodations even when an elected chief and council have been used. As is often said in Gitxaała discussions, "The council runs the reserve, but the smgigyet have authority over the laxyuup."

This chapter follows the lead of those smgigyet and community members who met in April 2008 to discuss and plan for a modern integrated system of Gitxaała governance. I begin with the historical authority to govern—the link between hereditary names and places. Out of this authority emerged the classical Gitxaała model of governance (the system most typically discussed in anthropology). I then consider how this system has been altered since the arrival of the K̲'amksiwa̲h (white people, and more generally non-Indigenous newcomers) and what has remained central to Gitxaała's systems and principles of governance. Underlying this discussion is the fact that through changing contexts Gitxaała's system of governance has maintained an integral core connected to the ancient past.

Authority to Govern Rooted in Place

The history of Gitxaała is told from the viewpoint of named people, who are members of the hereditary leadership. The setting within which these histories are told is public. Sometimes these people stand up alone to speak, but more often they stand in the company of a small number of siblings or with larger groups of their extended family. Each history focuses on the experiences of a particular named individual who is located by kinship in a social world and by actions and travel to a physical world. The social and physical worlds come together in this individual's history, providing the historical explanation for the customs and laws governing Gitxaała society.

Names, especially the names of hereditary leaders, are a critical aspect of Gitxaała's system of governance. Names are linked through historical events and experiences to particular places and encounters with human and nonhuman social beings. The authority and jurisdiction held by named hereditary leaders are thus rooted in the history of the ancestors who had the name previously.

According to the Gitxaała *adaawx* (oral record), the village of Lach Klan has been continuously inhabited by the Gitxaała since long before the arrival of Europeans on what is now known as the coast of British Columbia.[2] The following examples were recorded by William Beynon: "Then these men departed, and Tsibasa returned to his central village at Laxlan [Lach Klan]" ("The Origin of the Name He:l," 1916); "The Kitkatla had established a village at Laxklan for their feasts and winter ceremonials" ("The Tlingit Attack the Kitkatla," Nathan Shaw [Gitxaała], 1952); "The people went down to the water's edge and they again moved, and they found some other people at Laxklan, and here they remained until the present day" ("The Sky Brothers," Sam Lewis [Gitxaała], 1916).[3] In the adaawx recorded by Beynon and in contemporary oral accounts reference is made to the antiquity of the Gitxaała as an aboriginal community prior to the arrival of Europeans. Throughout my field research with Gitxaała in various settings, ranging from public meetings to informal conversations, Lach Klan has been clearly and consistently mentioned and discussed as the ancient center of Gitxaała.

In Beynon's unpublished "Ethnical and Geographical Study of the Tsimshian Nation" he contextually dates the existence of Lach Klan to the time before Ts'ibasaa came down the Skeena River: "When T'sibaesae and his Gispowudada group came down the Skeena from T'amlax'aem they went to where there were already some of the laxsk'ik (Eagle) group in Lax K'laen. . . . This was a gathering place where these people had their elevation feasts and where they held their feasts."[4]

The adaawx of the Sky Brothers documents a series of atrocities and subsequent movements of one of the lineages of Gitxaała. In this adaawx we learn of the trials and travels of Wudinuxs, a house leader of the Gitxaała Ganhada clan. This account took place before a significant flood event.

The "Flood" or "deluge," so called by many of Beynon's early respondents and by Gitxaała today, was likely a major earthquake that occurred several millennia ago. New archaeological evidence indicates a large flood or tsunami prior to two thousand years ago. Andrew Martindale's research team has found silt layers indicating a flood that, in the absence of direct dating, is estimated to have occurred between 3,500 and 5,000 years ago.[5] A similar silt layer has been found in a core sample from Shawatlan Cove in Prince Rupert Harbor (Eldridge and Parker 2007). These archaeological data corroborate accounts in the adaawx of a significant flood and allow for the conclusion that adaawx that reference the flood significantly predate European arrival.

After the flood Wudinuxs and his people "went down along the coast farther south, until they reached Bank's Island. Here they lived together as one household. Later they went to another place, until they came to the Kitkatla village at the end of Pitt Island known as Wilhahlgamilramedik (where the grizzly plays along the shore), and they lived there.[6] While there, the waters began to rise and come into the houses. The people anchored on a rock which the water had not covered. There they stayed for a long time; until the water went away suddenly, and they were on a mountain on Bank's Island, Laxgyiyaks. The people went down to the water's edge and they again move, and they found some other people at Laxklan, and here they remained until the present day" (Beynon notebook, 1916, BF 419).

Evidence for the antiquity of Gitxaała can also be found in the accounts of nonaboriginal merchants and traders who visited Gitxaała territory in the late 1700s. James Colnett, skipper of the British merchant ship *Prince of Wales*,[7] is acknowledged to be the first European to enter Gitxaała territory. Colnett and his crew met Seax (Shakes), a leading member of a Gispuwada house, and Sabaan, a house leader of a Gitxaała Ganhada house, in 1787, at the south end of Banks Island, a portion of the Gitxaała's southern territory. Some time after this initial meeting Colnett was invited to a *yaawk* (feast) in the company of Ts'ibasaa, the leading Gitxaała chief of the day, in accordance with Gitxaała *ayaawx* (customary law) (Galois 2004; see also Brown 1992). The *yaawk* or feast (variant potlatch) is a central social institution among the Gitxaała; it is a public event linked to, among other things, the passing of hereditary names, recognition of people, declarations of ownership, and formalization of alliances and agreements.

In 1792 the Spanish skipper Jacinto Caamano participated in a Gitxaała yaawk, as described by Susan Marsden (2007, 179–80; for a translation of the original journal of Don Jacinto Caamano, see Wagner and Newcombe 1938):

> Jacinto Caamano's vessel, anchored near the south end of Pitt Island, was approached by Homts'iit, a Raven clan chief of the Kitkatla tribe who danced the peace dance for him. He and his people were invited on board. Homts'iit gave Caamano the gift of an otter skin and Caamano served refreshments, after which Homts'iit exchanged names with Caamano, making them allies. Three weeks later Caamano attended a feast at Tuwartz Inlet [Citeyats].[8] Caamano described a series of feasting events in considerable detail, the first of which took place on August 28, when Homts'iit visited the ship to invite Caamano to a feast. Since the main elements in these ceremonial invitations are a peace dance and a *naxnox* [supernatural being] demonstration, the feathers to which Caamano refers were probably eagle down, the symbol of peace, and his various masks probably represented his various *naxnox* powers.

In 1795 the American skipper of the ship *Ruby*, Charles Bishop, described his meetings with Gitxaała people. Most notable is his repeated reference to "Shakes" (Sm'ooygit Seax), the Gitxaała "Huen Smokett (Great Chief)" (Roe 1967, 65–72, 90–93). Bishop notes the importance of locating himself within Sm'ooygit Seax's domains:

As Shake's dominions are very Extensive and Contain many good Harbours and inlets, the Principle business is to look out for one near the residence of the Chief as in the Situation you are shure of Procuring the Furs of the whole Tribe, and in this respect the Season must be consulted, for they shift their Habitations often, we having fell in with several evacuated villages. In the Spring and Early in the Summer the natives are found near the outside coast for taking halibut and other Ground fish, but when the Salmon go up the Freshes to Spawn they shift to the narrows and falls for Procuring their winters Stock of this delicious food. (Roe 1967, 72)

Throughout the early 1800s European fur traders and merchant sailors referred to Gitxaała as Sebassa Indians, after the ranking Sm'ooygit Ts'ibasaa (Dee 1945; Tolmie 1963). Gitxaała traders are recorded from north of Port Simpson on the north coast to Fort McLaughlin (present-day Bella Bella) to the south. Hudson Bay Company personnel describe Gitxaała as the dominant force in this region.

These early visits by Europeans to Gitxaała territory occurred in the context of a preexisting social order. The Gitxaała people were in place and had long-established laws, protocols, rules of ownership, and rights of use. In both Colnett's (Galois 2004, 138–66) and Caamano's (Wagner and Newcombe 1938, 269–93) logbooks and the adaawx of the Gitxaała can be found descriptions of the Europeans attempting to take things from Gitxaała territory and being rebuffed by the Gitxaała. A people well organized and confident in their authority and jurisdiction met Europeans beginning in the late 1700s. They greeted these early visitors with hospitality. European ships' logs describe the ceremony and festivities they encountered when they entered Indigenous territories. However, these European visitors did not fully appreciate—or perhaps they consciously rejected—Gitxaała laws and protocols.

Near the ancient village of Ks'waan (located at the southeastern tip of Banks Island), for example, Colnett and his crew were greeted by Seaxs and Ts'ibasaa in what appears to be a traditional greeting. Colnett was welcomed to laxyuup Gitxaała and told who were the rightful owners of the anchorage where he had secured his vessels and who owned the fish, timber, wild game, berries, and other foods and materials that his crew was gathering as if all was to be freely taken. When Colnett's crew's continued to harvest without paying compensation, Gitxaała people began to extract compensation, as was their right according to Gitxaała protocols.

Colnett further aggravated the situation by instructing his crew to continue harvesting food, timber, and supplies and to take offensive action when they felt under attack. In one particularly egregious act, a longboat was dispatched to ambush a group of Gitxaała who were in the act of preparing a meal. Colnett's crew killed three people (two men and one women) and then kidnapped and sexually assaulted the surviving women of the ambushed group (Galois 2004, 158–62). Despite (or perhaps because of) Colnett's continued aggressions, Gitxaała insisted on their authority and jurisdiction with laxyuup Gitxaała.

This historical documentation of ancient and more recent Gitxaała presence within the laxyuup defines the social organization of the classical model of governance.

Governance: The Classical Model

Indigenous governance systems are often studied and discussed as though they emerged sui generis out of the primordial depths. Likewise change and history are seen as products of the maelstrom of colonial intrusions and as representing decay and disruption. Obviously the colonization of Gitxaała and adjoining Indigenous territories was disruptive. However, it was not the moment that History began, nor does it portend a necessary collapse.

Gitxaała is a kin-ordered society; that is, the primary and essential social relations are defined in terms of who is related to whom and in what manner. Property, social rights, and place of residence—all the critical aspects of life—are governed by the nature of one's kin relations. Among Gitxaała family group membership is defined matrilineally; one belongs to a specific kin group called a *walp* (house group) based on who one's mother is. The father's side too is important, as it brings certain attributes and performs particular functions at key moments in life. But as Nees Ma'Outa states, "My concern lies more with my nephews than my own children" (Menzies and Butler 2011, 235).

Individual walp membership exists within an interacting set of social institutions: clan affiliation, social class, and village residence. Each social institution, or way of organization, has specific and important implications for being Gitxaała and for the governance of Gitxaała society and territory.

Each individual (with the exception, in the past, of slaves) belongs to one of four clans: Ganhada (raven), Gispuwada (blackfish), Laskiik (eagle), or Laxgibu (wolf). Clans do not exercise any specific political authority. That authority rests with the sm'ooygit and house groups. Clan affiliation, reckoned matrilineally, does inform who can marry whom and, consequently, alliances between members of specific house groups.

Historically three or four classes can be identified: high-ranking title holders and other title holders; freeborn commoners without rights to hereditary names; and slaves, those born to slaves or captured in war.

Members of the title-holding classes formed the hereditary leadership of Gitxaała. They are the smgigyet ("real people") or chiefs with rights and responsibility with respect to other community members. The origins of a sm'ooygit's right to governance can be found in the adaawx and is often linked to an event in which an ancestor received a gift or privilege from the spirit world, through political conquest, or through an alliance with another community. These histories link names to specific places, placing territories upon the house in the same way that a blanket is placed upon a chief when he takes on a name. The linkage between place, adaawx, and hereditary name is so important that a chief whose land is diminished or destroyed by, say, industrial logging or an oil spill becomes impoverished and loses status.

Titles, or hereditary names, are an important aspect of Gitxaała social organization. Hereditary names are passed along from one generation to the next through the feast system. Hereditary names are linked to, among other things, histories, crest images, territory, rights, and responsibilities. Not every Gitxaała person has a hereditary name, nor are all Gitxaała eligible to take on a hereditary name. Hereditary names exist throughout time, with different individuals having or taking on the name. For example, from the time several millennia ago that the high-ranking Gitxaała hereditary leader Sm'ooygit Ts'ibasaa left Temlax'am, through to the Ts'ibasaa of the early twentieth century, this name has existed as a social role that has been taken up by a line of successors.

Temlax'am (variant Temlaham; also Prairie Town) is an ancient village in what is today Gitxsan territory. In the old times, long before European contact, the people were dispersed from Temlax'am as a result of a series of disasters. Key Gispuwada houses and lineages, which are now Gitxaała, had their origins in Temlax'am.

Ownership of, access to, and rights of use of resource-gathering locations were and largely are governed by the walp. Notwithstanding the prominence of a paramount sm'ooygit or leader at the village level, the effective source of political power and authority with respect to the territory rests with the house leaders. This social unit is the political building block of the Gitxaała and Ts'msyen villages. The walp and the house territories, situated around natural ecosystem units such as watersheds, form the backbone of each village's collective territory.

Villages consist of groups of related and allied house groups who traditionally wintered together at a common site. While there have been some changes following the arrival of Europeans (for example, Lax Kw'alaams consists of members of what were formerly nine separate social groups with resource-harvesting territories along the Skeena River), the Gitxaała village of Lach Klan has been continuously inhabited before and after Europeans first arrived in their territories. Within the village there is a paramount sm'ooygit who is the house leader of the most powerful house group in the dominant clan. This person has traditionally wielded much power and economic wealth within the village; nonetheless his authority resides in the power and prestige of his house group.

In Gitxaała society the leading sm'ooygit, as elsewhere in the Tsimshianic world, "can expect constant and liberal economic support from his tribesmen" (Garfield 1939, 182). As Halpin and Seguin (1990, 276) note, "The village chief was the chief of the highest-ranking house in the village, and the other houses, in all clans, were ranked under him in descending order. . . . Traditional narratives report that the Southern Tsimshian [which would include Gitxaała] chiefs received tribute in the form of the first sea otter and seal caught by each canoe of sea hunters and other fur animals captured by land animals."

The importance of paying respect to the leading sm'ooygit underscores the recognition that the highest ranked sm'ooygit had a special place in the order of governance. This was not a position that entitled the sm'ooygit unfettered control over others of lower rank; it was, however, a structure that highlights the social and political acceptance by Gitxaała people that they were linked politically and socially through history, geography, and relations to one another in a way that set them apart from other Tsimshianic people. This structure also created the potential for a more coherent form of political alliance, such as began to emerge at or just prior to the arrival of the first Europeans in Gitxaała territory at the end of the 1770s.

Governance: In the Time of K̲'amksiwa̲h

When Colnett's crew ambushed, raped, and kidnapped Gitxaała people in 1787 he was setting in play a pattern that has shaped Indigenous-K̲'amksiwa̲h relations ever since. Though something of a different order, the deleterious effects of European arrival also includes the waves of disease that plagued the northwest coast from the 1700s to today. From early epidemics of smallpox, measles, and flu (which devastated coastal populations at near genocidal levels) to the modern diseases of diabetes, obesity, and heart disease (which are products, in part, of the colonial state's criminalization of Gitxaała practices of resource management),[9] Gitxaała and other Indigenous communities have faced enormous challenges maintaining their place and way in the world. Despite the forces of direct and passive aggression, Gitxaała people have persisted. As the Gitxaała world changed with the arrival of the K̲'amksiwa̲h the system of governance adapted to the new conditions, embedding new practices within ancient traditions.

Eric Wolf (1999, 123, 130) explains how the dual impact of disease and the penetration capitalist relations of production created a moment of cultural malaise in which the Kwakwaka'wakw's cosmological understanding of their world and their attendant system of governance morphed from an ideology of chiefly power into an ethnic or cultural identity. Wolf advances his argument by first outlining the extent and context of anthropological research conducted with the Kwakiutl. He takes care to caution his readers that "to think of the Kwakiutl as bearers of a changeless cultural pattern is inappropriate, since their existential conditions have changed in many ways since the time of first contact on the coast in 1774" (74). Not least was the cataclysmic population decline—a "demographic disaster" (77).

Population decline combined with the rise of a new capitalist economy that severed producers from the products of their labor and rewarded individuals in ways that undermined Kwakwaka'wakw lineage groups. "As epidemics killed off increasing numbers of legitimate incumbents to political and ritual positions, the enhanced opportunities and burdens of rank intensified pressure and tensions among the survivors" (Wolf 1999, 77). Participation in the capitalist economy created opportunities for those without rank or standing to gain wealth and thereby enter the competition for taking on the hereditary names left empty. Hereditary leaders, for their part, tried to maintain their position by elevating those who in other times would never have been considered. As Wolf goes on to say, this led to an inherent contradiction in the Kwakiutl system of governance that contributed to the cultural malaise in which the cosmological underpinnings of the chiefly order fell apart. From the ashes of the chiefly ideology emerged an ethnic identity that allowed the survivors to claim a space within the context of the modern pluralist state.

While I find aspects of this argument compelling and can see some reflection in the contemporary practices and sentiments in Gitxaała, it is to a certain extent an overstating of the case in the context of Gitxaała. The depopulation of Gitxaała communities did have an impact on how survivors of the onslaught of epidemics responded and organized themselves. The archaeological record reveals changes in regional use and occupation throughout Gitxaała laxyuup from around the mid-1800s. Community members recall to this day the effects of these nineteenth-century epidemics and talk of mass burials of the victims. Throughout this time hereditary names were temporarily set aside as those left alive consolidated the high-ranking names and house groups to ensure their survival into the future.

Most of the population decline appears to have begun in the early nineteenth century (but there are clear accounts of earlier waves of death), just prior to the penetration of fully formed capitalist relations of production through the development of the fish canning industry and then forestry soon thereafter. Archaeological surveys that I have conducted in Gitxaała territory show that most permanent year-round abandonment of the major villages outside of Lach Klan occurred in the early nineteenth century. We can tell this from the age of the second-growth trees in these sites, from oral accounts of abandonment of primary residential locations, from European records, and from the use of archaeological dating techniques. Along with the changes to the material and social landscape came changes to Gitxaała's system of governance, changes that melded old and new and sustained Gitxaała as a unique people.

A new Gitxaała system of governance emerged out of the encounter with K̲'amksiwah. The fact that this encounter was a transformative moment is recorded in the oral history. In the context of meeting with James Colnett, Ts'ibasaa held a feast to welcome this new chief to Gitxaała laxyuup. After visiting Colnett's ships the people returned to their village.

> When the Gitxaała people reached their village, Ts'ibasaa said, "I will give a great feast [ne-amex, friendship-making ritual] and these people shall be my guests." When Ts'ibasaa gave this feast, he gave away to the guests many valuable furs, and so greatly pleased was the chief of these ghost people that among the presents they gave to the Gitxaała were guns and ammunition and they taught them how to use these, so that the Gitxaała were the first in the north to have guns and ammunition. They were the first to use it to hunt the fur seal and sea otter and were much dreaded by the other tribes. (Beynon notebook, 1953, interview with James Lewis, Gitxaała, BF 40.3, no. 61, CMC)

It was at this historical moment that Ts'ibasaa took up the name He:l, which persists today as the highest ranked Gitxaała name. In the course of the feast put on for the Ghost People, he gave names to their highly ranked people, the ship's captain and officers. Names were taken up from the Europeans as well.

He:l marks the early encounter between Gitxaała and the newcomers. He:l was not, however, a totally new name. For that matter neither was Sabaan, the chief who first saw the newcomers arriving, an ancient name but one that emerged out of this encounter as well.[10] Galois (2004, 269) published an extract of George McCauley's account of Sabaan receiving his name during a meeting with early K'amksiwah visitors. According to Galois, the original narrative was collected on February 9, 1916.[11] Upon close review of a copy of Beynon's 1916 Gitxaała field notebooks (vols. 1–6, BF 419–24, box 24, CMC), it is apparent that the pages with McCauley's account were removed from the original notebooks and filed by Barbeau separately. Notes are included from January 31 through February 8 and then from February 10 until the end of Beynon's visit in Lach Klan. It is not clear what other associated materials may have been removed from the notebook or how, in removing the pages, Barbeau may have altered the material record of Beynon's field trip. Other interview notes with McCauley remain in Beynon's 1916 field notebooks.

He:l was part of an older name, wiheld'm (underscore added), which was itself part of a longer name of a high-ranking nephew of Ts'ibasaa.[12] The earliest recorded account of the name He:l comes from Joshua Tsibassa in a series of interviews with Beynon in 1916. It is important to point out that the right to tell this account would have resided with Joshua Tsibassa, who, at that time, was the highest ranked sm'oogit of Gitxaała and the head of the house of He:l which by the early twentieth century had subsumed the houses of Seax and Ts'ibasaa both. Joshua Tsibassa, and the other smgigyet interviewed by Beynon in 1916, refer to the house of He:l as the highest ranking royal house in Gitxaała. As recorded by Beynon, the house of He:l contained five subdivisions: "Each of these subdivisions were made dependant houses in former times but were all of the same origin and same myths and crests as the head of the royal family He:l. When He:l came to Gitxaała the chief at that time being Wisa'ag [Seax], Gispawudwada [Gispuwada or Blackfish clan] a former brother of He:l at T'amlax'm and when He:l and his brothers came to Gitxaała they amalgamated with Wisa'ag who had the same names and crests having originally come from the same place as He:l" (Beynon notebook, 1916, BF 423, CMC).

Here we see the name He:l being used to refer to an ancient ancestor who had first arrived on the coast several millennia before Europeans and long before the short version of the name, He:l, came to be associated with that personage of Tsibassa.[13] Joshua Tsibassa would have been cognizant that he was using the name He:l to refer to the royal Gispuwada house, as would have been the other Gitxaała interviewed by Beynon in 1916. This acknowledges the special role and place of the name He:l in the transformation of Gitxaała politics and society through the encounter with colonial processes. Joshua Tsibassa continues to explain to Beynon the importance of the name He:l and its position in the contemporary context:

> This name was first given to Tsiybɛsɛ [Tsibassa] by a white man by the name of Capt. Hale. Capt. Hale upon visiting all of the other villages of Indians came until Tsiybɛsɛ and seeing the Gitxaała was the largest of the different villages he had visited gave his name to Tsiybɛsɛ who some time afterwards called a feast and applied the name Hale to wiheld'əm wildɛł nəkłəłstɔ'lt. The informant says that Capt. Hale was the first white man to see Gitxaała and the name He:l is of recent origin having originated at this event. Capt. Hale according to informant was an American (Boston) trader and explorer. The reason the name was applied to wiheld'əm was that the name "Hale" bore a close resemblance to wiheld'əm in sound and was applied in this case. (Beynon notebook, Gitxaała, 1916, vol. 1, BF 419, box B29, CMC)

Over the course of the nineteenth century the name He:l came to stand for the amalgamated high-ranked Gispuwada houses whose members controlled the maritime fur trade. (For an account of the early nineteenth-century Ts'ibasaa, see Mitchell 1981). By the end of the nineteenth century and the start of the twentieth He:l was the unequivocal name used to refer to this group of Gispuwada. The rise of He:l as synonymous with Ts'ibasaa is a critical act of transformation within Gitxaała that simultaneously respects Indigenous history and law and demonstrates Gitxaała's recognition of the changing world. Encapsulated within the transformation of the name from that of a high-ranked nephew of the head chief to the top-ranked name is a demonstration of active engagement with the newcomers and a testament to the continuity of traditional practices and intellectual frameworks. The value of the name was not simply in its being gifted from the Europeans; it was also connected to property and history within Gitxaała in the form of the nephew's existing name and to his ultimate inheritance of the territories held by the house of Ts'ibasaa and Seax. This historical account is part of an intellectual tradition of inquiry and classification that seeks to locate Europeans—Ḵ'amksiwah—within a Gitxaała model of society and to connect Gitxaała to the new Ḵ'amksiwah world.

He:l thus marks the arrival of Europeans within Gitxaała's world and the transformation of He:l into a position of preeminence within the hereditary system. Through the encounter with Europeans and then through the affirmation of the feasting system He:l came to subsume within it the prerogatives of the house of Ts'ibasaa and Seax— the two high lineages of the Gispuwada. He:l becomes Ts'ibasaa and Seax in a transformative act that holds history and territory together so that one can maintain the ability to govern in the present. This is the critical point here: even as the world changes, the hereditary system of governance is simultaneously adapting to the changes.

It is useful to return briefly to Wolf's (1999) analysis of the Kwakwaka'wakw through the lens of an earlier analysis of the Haisla by Pritchard (1977). Following a line of argumentation that anticipates Wolf's analysis, Pritchard suggests that in the transition to a modern capitalist economy based in fisheries and forestry the economic power and redistributional function played by lineage and house group chiefs were undermined and the relevance of trying to strictly maintain traditional chiefly governance was diminished. Thus, says Pritchard, "the time, effort, and feeling invested in the maintenance of clans and names are, I believe, an instance of a system operating on emotional momentum, divorced from the substantive underpinnings that once sustained it" (281). The Haisla lacked the rich sockeye streams that the late nineteenth-century commercial fishery was interested in. Their forestlands also lacked timber of sufficient economic value to sustain more than hand logging in the early twentieth century. (Later in the twentieth century the potential for hydroelectric generation and a deep sea harbor led to the development of an aluminum smelter and electrical power generation projects in Haisla territory.) This left the Haisla to their traditional territories without significant competition from capitalist firms; at the same time there were individual employment opportunities for Haisla people in Rivers Inlet to the south and the Skeena to the north. This situation removed the economic power of the chiefs while leaving the Haisla relatively unmolested on their land.

Gitxaała had a somewhat different situation. Here the chiefly prerogatives remained linked to economically productive territories. First, through their advantageous location on the outer coast and hence an early and monopoly-like access to maritime fur traders, Gitxaała smgigyet, like Ts'ibasaa, were able to retain and strengthen their lineage authority and the economic power on which their authority was based. As the commercial fishery emerged, Gitxaała smgigyet maintained an economic base to their power well into the early twentieth century thanks to having traditional territories based on small to medium-size sockeye watersheds, the relative isolation from the main commercial fisheries on the Skeena, and the ability to assert authority over access to these same fishing systems as a result of the power maintained through the fur trade.

It is perhaps a quirk of fate that Gitxaała's chiefly class retained an economic base to their power well into the twentieth century. During the early maritime fur trade (1787–1832) Gitxaała was strategically located and thus able to intercept trading vessels on their seaward coastline and simultaneously control the access to these traders by their inland neighbors. This provided lineage heads like Ts'ibasaa with the strategic advantage and material resources to hold onto power within Gitxaała and over a wider geographical stretch of the coast. The nearby Ts'msyen chiefly class (from the Skeena River), like the Kwakiutl to the south, found the material basis to their power slipping away. Legaic, a Ts'msyen sm'ooygit, held military control over access to the Hudson Bay Company trading post of Fort Simpson from about 1832 to 1862 (Marsden and Galois 1995). However, his apparent control over productive property, such as the sockeye salmon creeks within the estuary of the Skeena River, was quickly diminished when the industrial canners and the accompanying Canadian fisheries laws penetrated this region.

The rise of the industrial salmon canning industry in the Skeena River (circa 1877) served to undermine the economic power of the Ts'msyen chiefs to the north of Gitxaała while simultaneously strengthening Gitxaała smgigyet power. Commercial canning efforts focused on the Skeena River, the core of the Ts'msyen chief's territories. Consequently Canadian fisheries regulations were targeted on this region to ensure that the canners had untrammeled access to salmon. This was accomplished by criminalizing aboriginal fisheries practices. Meanwhile Gitxaała smgigyet had managed to secure their primary sockeye streams (sockeye being the species sought by the canners) through the assignment of reserves, by gaining control over local seine permits, and by the relative isolation of their sockeye streams.

While these small coastal sockeye systems were highly productive under Gitxaała management, they were relatively small systems compared to the millions of sockeye entering the Skeena River. The industrial canners focused on high volume and economic efficiencies. Gitxaała had sufficient labor power and capacity to operate their own fishing operations to sell fish to the Skeena River canneries and to put up supplies of non-commercially targeted salmon and other fish species. Unfortunately for the Ts'msyen, their fishing systems were right in the path of the large sockeye runs and in sites that the industrial firms wanted. With the help of the provincial and federal governments, these firms were able to take effective control over the Ts'msyen fishing locations. Gitxaała smgigyet thus retained control over productive property in the form of salmon creeks and the associated fishing permits well into the 1960s. This economic foundation supported and maintained a system of governance that remained rooted in smgigyet's connection to the laxyuup of their walp.

In 1882 BC Indian Reserve Commissioner Peter O'Reilly came to Lach Klan to meet with Gitxaała chiefs to set up reserves. O'Reilly met with Seax but was able to set up only three reserves at this meeting because Ts'ibasaa was not present. In Ts'ibasaa's absence Seax would not make any agreement over reserves beyond the village of Lach Klan, a cemetery near the village, and K'moda (Ts'ibasaa's own fishing station). A decade later, in 1891, O'Reilly was finally able to meet with Ts'ibasaa and a delegation of thirty chiefs when the balance of Gitxaała's reserves were established.

Over the course of the transition from the chiefly economy of ancient times to the industrial resource extraction capitalism of the late nineteenth century the jurisdiction and authority of the smgigyet remained a central component of Gitxaała governance. This is a critical point and an aspect of Gitxaała governance that persists to this day, even in the face of the government of Canada's continued attempts to mandate and enforce democratic individualism (the principle of one person one vote and elected corporate-style councils). As Gitxaała's system of governance developed a division of responsibility has emerged between the Band Council—which manages the reserve land base, including water, sewer, and on-reserve social services—and the hereditary leadership, who hold the authority and jurisdiction over the laxyuup Gitxaała.

Continuity amid Change

A century and a bit after meeting with O'Reilly Gitxaała members still insist on the importance of hereditary leadership. The linkage between hereditary name, the laxyuup of the walp, and the authority of the smgigyet remains strong. At the conclusion of the 2008 community governance workshop community members in Lach Klan affirmed in no uncertain terms that there were three foundational principles to Gitxaała governance: (1) adaawx (history) and ayaawx (law); (2) a well-functioning hereditary system; and (3) the council of smgigyet. This is very much as it was in 1891, when Gitxaała met with O'Reilly, and as it was in 1787, when Gitxaała met with Colnett. The world changes, the system adapts, but the underlying core retains the linkage between the real people and the land. Without that connection the very idea of Gitxaała might disappear.

3

Laxyuup

The Land and Ocean Territories of Gitxaała

Without territory, a sm'ooygit has no power. Without the ability to harvest, one does not have the ability to feast. Without the feast, names cannot be passed on. While much has changed since James Colnett first arrived in Gitxaała territory, one thing has remained strong: the importance of place and territory in the modern Gitxaała identity and way of life.

When people return to Lach Klan, family and friends say, "Welcome home." This is a sense of home that is more than just a reference to a small village or a family house. A cousin once asked me, in reference to a research project on poverty and homelessness in Gitxaała, "How can people be homeless here? This is their home, all of Gitxaała territory." Home is thus more than a physical place; it is a sentiment rooted in a real social and physical connection to the laxyuup, the land and ocean territories of Gitxaała. There are of course people with inadequate housing and people who face impoverished living conditions, yet all Gitxaała people have a home, the laxyuup Gitxaała. This chapter documents the extent of the laxyuup and how Gitxaała relations to and use of the laxyuup have shifted over the course of the past two centuries.

Gitxaała Traditional Territories

The terrestrial and marine areas that compose laxyuup Gitxaała extend from Ts'ibasaa's oolichan fishing territory on the Nass River south to the coastal islands just north of Kitasu Bay. This territory stretches seaward to the marine territories of the Haida Nation. To the east Gitxaała territory extends to the mainland shore of Grenville Channel and abuts the areas the Haisla and Hartley Bay communities now use.

Gitxaała's use of their traditional territory has undergone a significant centralization subsequent to the allocation of reserves by Peter O'Reilly in the late 1800s. As Gitxaała sigyidm hana'a Thelma Hill states, "There were so many little villages where the Gitxaała lived before they chose Lach Klan to live."[1] Gitxaała traditional territory is wide and noncontiguous, reflecting the precontact movements of people for harvesting, trading, and feasting and, later, the postcontact integration of new economic opportunities.

Gitxaała oral history emphasizes the primacy of the Gitxaała people on the coast. They differentiate themselves from the people known as Ts'msyen, who they believe arrived on the coast at a later time. While linguists, anthropologists, and colonial governments have put the Gitxaała in the general category of Tsimshian, the Gitxaała themselves have emphasized their distinct identity and origins. Their territorial claim throughout the north coast is linked to the nation's antiquity. "We were already occupying these areas," says Gitxaała sm'ooygit Matthew Hill, "and I think that is where we have to be very specific, because all the others just came and Gitxaała was always generous and accommodating people, no matter where within our territory."[2]

Gitxaała hereditary leaders and elders often describe their residence on the coast as predating "the Flood" and indicate particular locations where Gitxaała people anchored their vessels atop mountains. Beynon also documented adaawx of floods in his early twentieth-century interviews of Gitxaała people. Traces of cataclysmic floods, tsunamis, and other forms of localized inundations can be found in the archaeological and geological records. Taken together the material and oral records locate Gitxaała on the coast within the laxyuup many millennia ago.

Lach Klan has been continuously inhabited for over nine millennia as a central Gitxaała village. Even so it has not always been the primary center of the Gitxaała world in the way that it became in the postcontact period. Furthermore hereditary leaders and elders emphasize that Lach Klan is a particular place, while Gitxaała refers to the people and encompasses a much broader geography.

Gitxaała people had customary rights to and spent significant periods of time in places outside of the contemporary core territory associated with the village of Lach Klan and the larger coastal islands of Pitt, Banks, Campania, and the Estevan Group. Gitxaała oral history and the Northwest Coast ethnographic record include references to both close and distant sites to which Gitxaała lineages held rights through various forms of social relations and alliances. Mitchell and Donald (2001), discussing oolichan fishing sites on the BC coast, cite McIlwraith (1948, 359, 360), who documented that Gitxaała people traveled to the Kitlope to produce grease and that the high-ranking Gitxaała leader Ts'ibasaa sometimes remained there for the entire season.[3] The descendants of Ts'ibasaa and He:l continue to travel from Lach Klan to Haisla territory to participate in the oolichan harvest. The yearly movement of Gitxaała and Ts'msyen to sites on the Nass River for oolichan harvesting and grease making is also documented (see Mitchell and Donald 2001, 25).

Gitxaała territory can be thought of as the sum of the individual house territories plus the use areas that Gitxaała people access through their lineage groups that extend beyond the village polity. Lineages, rooted in common origin histories, irrespective of whether or not the specific house groups lived in the same primary village, shared rights to use their lineage relatives' territories. House territories and use areas of houses in the same lineages come together like a patchwork quilt that blankets the physical landscape in story, memory, and communities of shared practice. Taken in its entirety laxyuup Gitxaała is an expansive place that occupies much of what now constitutes the north coast of British Columbia.

Colonialism, Reserves, and Understanding the Laxyuup

The territorial boundaries used more recently by twentieth-century colonial governing structures (for example, the Department of Fisheries and Oceans) reflect significant changes in seasonal movements of Gitxaała people and a process of residential centralization forced upon the Gitxaała by colonial economic and political pressures. Representations of Gitxaała's territories by these agencies are tinged by contemporary intentions, not historical accuracy. As was noted in chapter 1, even contemporary academic representations of the people and the laxyuup have been unduly influenced by contemporary political conflicts. In particular the orthodoxy promulgated by archaeologists working in Prince Rupert Harbor have unfortunately and inaccurately invented a Northern Coast–Tsimshian people living to the north of the mouth of the Skeena River, even though the archaeological evidence cannot support their contention and the oral literature suggests an alternative understanding (see chapter 1). This section explores the ways in which history, political processes, and Indigenous agency have shaped contemporary usage in the context of the creation of the reserve system.

The imposition of the Canadian Fisheries Act in the late 1800s (Lutz 2008; Newell 1993) and the British Columbia Wildlife Act (Lutz 2008, 147, 248) and the subsequent criminalization of aboriginal food harvesting and resource management practices have infringed upon the capacity and practices of Gitxaała community members to access the full extent of the laxyuup. This situation intensified over the last third of the twentieth century following the cancelation of drag seine permits operated by community members since the late 1800s at key Gitxaała fishing locations.

For contemporary community members there is an intensive harvesting and use zone near the village (Butler 2004). This is a space that many general-purpose harvesters access. Other, more specialized and active harvesters continue to utilize the full extent of Gitxaała's territory. However, government agencies and casual observers often misinterpret generalist use patterns as indicators of the extent of the traditional territories without understanding the nature or the importance of the larger traditional territory in the ongoing practice of the hereditary system. That system is linked to resource use but extends far beyond material use to the use of the territory as a symbolic manifestation of Gitxaała's history, linked through named hereditary leaders and their house territories.

Consultants hired to defend their clients' legal incursions into Gitxaała laxyuup have used reserve locations to demarcate traditional territories. In litigation on behalf of the federal government and their community allies, these consultants have attempted to construct an argument that would constrain and restrict the territorial extent of

Gitxaała's laxyuup. Their contention is that the reserve allocations define a contiguous territory that best maps onto a customary idea of the ancient territorial boundaries and aboriginal polity. This approach ignores the relevance of the linkage between history, name, and territory for Gitxaała, drawing instead from a Eurocentric perspective. At the same time as this approach ignores the cultural protocols of Gitxaała it also denies the agency of late nineteenth-century Gitxaała smgigyet, who were actively making strategic economic decisions on their community's behalf.

For example, in the late 1880s and early 1890s Paul Sebassah (Sm'ooygit Ts'ibasaa) was pivotal in establishing reserves for Gitxaała, Hartley Bay (Gitga'ata), and Metlakatla. Sebassah was a prominent leader of William Duncan's Christian community at Metlakatla. Duncan was concerned that settlers were usurping aboriginal fishing rights and convinced Indian Reserve Commissioner O'Reilly to visit the north coast. According to Duncan, "Indian fisheries were being taken possession of by whites for cannery purposes, and . . . if steps were not taken to secure to the Indians their fisheries, they would suffer great injustice" (Inglis 2011, 5). O'Reilly visited in 1881 and returned to "the North Coast in 1882, 1888, 1891, and 1893 to continue the allotment of Indian Reserves" (5).

In order to understand Sebassah's role one needs to appreciate that as Sm'ooygit Ts'ibasaa he was not only the ranking hereditary leader among Gitxaała but the unrivaled hereditary leader of the coastal Tsimshianic peoples. Thus he played a central role in negotiating reserves not only for Gitxaała but also for Metlakatla and Gitga'ata. Sebassah drew from his local position of power in Metlakatla and his role as sm'ooygit in Gitxaała to ensure that Gitxaała prerogatives were maintained as he negotiated.

Only three reserves were set during O'Reilly's first meeting with Gitxaała: Lach Klan (Indian Reserve [IR] 1), Grassy Island, a graveyard (IR 2), and Sebassah's own house territory, K'moda (IR 3). O'Reilly arrived while Sebassah was out of the community. Not until O'Reilly was able to meet with Sebassah in person—at K'moda, Sebassah's traditional fishing site, in 1891—was O'Reilly able to discuss setting up addition reserves for Gitxaała.

I held a long conference with "She-aks" [Seax] the 2nd Chief, and some of the tribe, the principal Chief "Sebassa" and many of his people being absent, engaged in sea otter hunting. "She-aks" stated that the tribe had held several meetings to consider what land would be necessary for them, and gave me the names of the numerous places they wished for, many of which were on Islands far out at sea, and which could not be visited at that time of year, without the aid of a Steamer, and as it was impracticable for me to engage one for this service, I was reluctantly compelled to abandon the idea of completing the Reserves for this tribe until some future opportunity. The following plots were however, subsequently allotted after the usual conversation with the Indians present.

No. 1. Dolphin Island, on which the winter village of Kitlathla stands contains about two thousand seven hundred (2700) acres, and is situated in an exposed position on Hecate Channel, between Queen Charlotte Islands, and the mainland. This is a bleak barren tract of country, stocked with scrub timber which is only fit for fuel. . . . The village is very conveniently situated to some of the best halibut and herring fisheries and is within easy reach of the waters most frequented by the fur seal and sea otter. Nowhere on the Coast is game more abundant, deer, bear, and wildfowl being especially numerous. . . .

No. 2. Grassy Islet lying one mile North of the Village, contains one (1) acre, and is used only as a burial ground.

No. 3. "Kum-o-wa-dah" situated at the No. 3 waterfall at the head of Lowe Inlet, contains one hundred and ninety (190) acres; this is perhaps one of the most valuable Salmon fisheries that I have met with on the Coast.[4]

When O'Reilly eventually met with Sebassah, on July 10, 1891 the final reserves (described by O'Reilly as fishing stations) were set up. O'Reilly met with Sebassah, Seax, and "over 30 Inds." at the Lowe Inlet Cannery (Inglis 2011, 8). Though O'Reilly does not name the "over 30 Inds." it is very likely they were the ranking hereditary leaders and title holders responsible for the fishing stations that he assigned as reserves. The establishment of these reserves is clearly tied to ensuring ongoing and legally guaranteed access to the salmon fishery. This is not a process of establishing the customary boundaries or the fullest extent of the traditional territory of Gitxaała. Furthermore each of these fishing stations is also a sockeye salmon creek. At this stage of the commercial cannery fishery sockeye was the prime species of harvest. Thus Gitxaała fishers needed to protect and control access to these sockeye streams. They could pursue fishing on dog, pink, coho, and spring salmon streams relatively untrammeled by Canadian government enforcement, which ignored all but sockeye at that time. This further suggests that the establishment of these reserves was focused on access to the expanding commercial salmon fishery, in which Gitxaała people were playing a critical role as labor and fishermen; it was not about defining the extent of Gitxaała traditional territories.

The impact of European trading, settlement, and industrial development in the region did alter Gitxaała and Tsimshian settlement and harvesting patterns. In the areas surrounding what is now known as Prince Rupert, changes to settlement patterns were immense. The contemporary village of Lax Kw'alaams is located at a Hudson Bay Company fort site established in 1834. Members of nine tribes whose traditional territories were closer to the Skeena River settled this site subsequent to the establishment of Fort Simpson. The village of Metlakatla, an older Gitxaała settlement site, was repopulated in 1862 by Christian converts following the missionary William Duncan. Joshua Tsibassa, a leading sm'ooygit at the turn of the nineteenth century, identified Metlakatla as a Gitxaała site in a narrative collected by Beynon, titled "The Myth of the Adventures of Gom'asnext": "Years ago many people lived at Metlakatla and it was [where] Nagapt of Gitxala lived. And this is why the Gitxala lived here."[5] Winter village sites such as Lach Klan and postcontact villages such as Lax Kw'alaams have become the focus of contemporary discussions of tribal territories, but traditional, precontact territories included sites of occupation and use much farther dispersed than the contemporary village polity.

The Land and Waters of the Gitxaała
as Recorded by Beynon in 1916

Beynon provides a unique glimpse into the nature and extent of
Gitxaała's core territory in the early twentieth century. Beynon, who
had met the Canadian anthropologist Marius Barbeau at Port Simpson
in 1915, was a Tsimshian of the wolf clan. He had been educated in Victoria and went north in 1915 to find work. Barbeau arrived in Port Simpson to conduct research and found in Beynon an able researcher; they
would go on to forge a lifelong working relationship.

Barbeau hired Beynon in 1916 to continue research on his behalf in
Gitxaała. Barbeau's instructions to Beynon were to record the hunting
grounds of the Gitxaała: "You may first study the outlines of the tribe,
its geographic position on the map, its former stations, hunting grounds,
territory: the royal and councilors' families, the individual names and
translations, the crests, and the related myths and the origins of families of the tribe."[6]

Barbeau seems to have assumed that the hunting grounds were the
same as the totality of the laxyuup Gitxaała. However, that assumption is not warranted. First, we can see from the historic record of a
century earlier that under Ts'ibasaa, Gitxaała's jurisdiction, authority, and political influence extended much farther to the south than
Beynon records in his 1916 notebooks. Additionally the origin history of an important and ancient Blackfish lineage locates their lineage home on the Moore Islands off the coast of Aristazabal Island.
Furthermore Barbeau's directions focus Beynon's attention on a narrow range of uses of the territory: hunting and activities related there-
to. Yet despite Barbeau's shortcomings, Beynon's descriptions and
commentary from 1916 provide a useful look at the core Gitxaała territory circa 1916.

Beynon describes the hunting territories of Gitxaała as reported to
him during his first visit to the village of Lach Klan, and he describes
the four Gitxaała clans (which he identifies as phratries):

A village situated on the extreme north west end of Dolphin Island, having at present [1916] two hundred and fifty inhabitants.

The main industry of these people is fishing and trapping. They have no divisions as to tribes. . . . They differ from the Port Simpson who are divided into tribes. . . . The Gitxała people are only divided into phratrays Ganhada, Gispawudwada, Laxskiok, Laxkibo each one having its royal chiefs and houses. But hEl of Gispawudwada royal house is the recognized chief of the Gitxała people who in former years held a position next to the Port Simpson . . . Tsimyen and were very powerful in war. . . . [Gitxaała] still adhere to ancient ceremonies. (Beynon notebook, 1916, BF 419.1, CMC)

He also lists Gitxaała houses:

The Gitxała village was composed of the following houses in order of rank.[7] . . . Royal Gispawudwada . . . house of hEl which is the head of the following subdivisions who all had independent houses. The chief before hEl came to Gitxała was wis'aj gisp who hEl on his arrival from Temlar'am became amalgamated to this house and afterwards became chief and remained so up to the present day but is divided into the following subdivisions
   1. Tsiybese 2. Niesno'ł 3. Nieswe'xs 4. Gunaxno'tk 5. Txagexs 6 Niesłkuxso'
   II Royal house Gisp. of Gitxała seks who is subdivided into the following who each were independent house (The former chief name of this house was dxe'enk) 1. niesgamdxowe 2. 'awe'sdi 3. waxáit
   The royal Ganhada 1. exłewels 2. wi'nemo'lk 3. wak .es (watsta) 4. dopxxen
   These four were of one group of Ganhada chiefs another group 1. ladox 2. hamdxi 3. ados 4. nios'ayaim
   The Laxskiok and Laxkibo have no royal houses. (Beynon notebook, 1916, BF 419.1, CMC)

In the process of his research among the Gitxaała, Beynon documented "all their (Gitxaała) hunting territories before . . . most . . . informants go away" (1916, BF 422.10). He includes both a description of the territories (land and water) and identification of whom the various locations belonged to. A map accompanies the written description of the territories.

Beynon identified the individuals he spoke with as Joshua Tsibassa, Samuel Lewis, Albert Argyle, and Job Spencer. What follows is his record of their identification of the significant territories of the Gitxaała:

> The territory of the royal house of hel Gispawudwada was on Pitt Island and I have marked 1. This was known as ktsim'alagam . . . and here was gathered the salmon and berries and was also a hunting grounds. It also extended onto the mainland and this was the property of this royal house and all its subdivisions. Hel also had another territory but this was used by all the Gitxala and here in olden times was the village of wisa'ag at the north end of Pitt Island marked 2 and was called wilhatga'amilga medi'k "where the grizzly plays along the shore." And next to this was the territory of nias'ois gispawadwuda marked 3. This place was known as kta'ol . . . and here was the hunting grounds of this house and next to this was the territory of the house of 'nagap't ganhada marked 4. This place was known as k'tai and here was gathered berries and salmon and on the mainland across from Pitt Island was the property of the royal house of seks known as kmodo (Lowe Inlet) marked 5 and the seks also had another place on Pitt Island known as kne'mujam ba'alx. This was a berry picking ground . . . marked 6 and next the territory of the seks was the territory belonging to the ganhada house of dxagamfishaitks known as gan'a'ol (Bear pit hap.) marked 7 . . . This was on the end of Kennedy Island marked 8. (Beynon notebook, Gitxaała, B-F-422.10, CMC)

> And the property of nagwitogem laxe ganhada had as his territory upon which this house gathered berries and fish in the river and was also the hunting grounds known as sqaskin'is. . . . This was marked 9. And this was the property of the Laxgibo house of łebeksk and this was known as gaipoł. . . . Marked 10. At the South End of Pitt island was the village of 'extewels royal ganhada and

was known as dxowenxtom galdzep (The village in the Point) marked 11. And adjoining this was the territory known as dxim wilu nek ". . . Inlet" This is marked 12. And then on Pitt Island nias'ois had two places territories and the second one was known as gal'atgao (wetsta word. Meaning?) marked 13. the Gitxała village of Laxklen (present village) where all the people lived during the winter marked 14. And then the territory of ayaigansk . . . marked 15. (BF 423.1)

And on MacCauley Island there is the territory gushawel Gispawudwada and was known as 'nisek'wat'se "Place where sling shots were made," marked as 16. And on this island was another territory belonging to the Gispawudwada house of watali known as tkulaxlax "around falling" named on account of the steep sides of the island and was the trap set for animals . . . marked, 17. And . . . part of Porcher Island was the territory of wa'omxk Gispawudwada known as witunaxno'x. This place of supernatural beings marked No. 18. and there the property of nioshalopas Laxskiok . . . known as kspinałe marked 19. (BF 423.1)

On Banks Island was the property of la'ol ganhada known as gitgiyeks "The people way out to sea," marked 20. Adjoining this was the property of gaiyemtkwe Gispawudwada known as nego'a'ks ("water splashing against") on account of the rough water splashing against the steep cliffs and on this account was given this name, marked 21. And then adjoining this was the territory of lutkudzemti laxski'k known as laxsto'ltem dodzep "on Beaver Cliff." This cliff was a Fort and was made on a high cliff. 22. And on the south end of Banks Island was the territory of the ganhada royal house of 'wakés and it was known as k'manxata, so called because at the extreme point was a sheltered bay and was always calm. Xata means calm inlet. . . . Marked No. 23. (BF 423.1)

Campania Island was the territory of nias'oio and niaslo's and on the S.E. end of the Island was nugun'aks the island itself was known as laxgitgiyeks "on the people of island at sea" 24. (BF 423.1)

Territories of the Gitxala . . . Another territory which was used by all the Gitxala people and was a place that they camped at when on their way to the Nass River where in early part of the year they would go and get the oolichan fish and they had camps all the way up. This was one of them and was known as kso'naoks—Long Point (Just south of the cannery known as Claxton), marked 25. (BF 423.1)

And at Porcher Island the Ganhada and Gispawudwada people had all to themselves where they would always hunt. The gisp. territory was known as k'pexł marked 26. And the Ganhada peoples territory was known as gaswe'not tibon . . . marked 27. And on the Nass River the people also had another place which all used (Gitxała) and here they gathered grease and oolichan. It was known as samq'łe'ala (Real old seal). . . . Marked 28. (BF 423.1)

Gitxaała narratives (for example, the "Myth of Crest of gaiyemtkwe"), as recorded by Beynon in 1916, refer to Banks Island:

Myth of Crest of gaiyemtkwe: the crest hagwiejem giyeks (The monster a way out to sea). Told by A. Argyle. Feb. 14/16. This house was a house of hunters and they hunted chiefly the sea otter (p'ton). . . . They went all the time to one place known as laxgiyeks (in sea away out) (a long way out from Bank's Island). (BF 421.8)

I asked informant [A. Argyle, Feb. 14/16] if he could give me any information on the house of 'extewels royal ganhada. Informant states that they have been extinct a long time but he heard his grandmother state they were of the same group as having at one time lived at gadu' and were of gidaganitz origin and from these they came on to the Gitxala after the flood. For in the songs of this house they sing of how they were at gadu' and how they drifted out to sea and found a rock here they anchored and when the waters receded they found they were on Banks Island. (BF 421.9)

Beynon's records of these hunting territories and associated Gitxaała house groups provide an intriguing portrait of the use and occupancy of Gitxaała a century and a half after Colnett and Caamano arrived at the laxyuup. It is evident that the century of depopulation by disease and the economic disruption caused by the newcomers had worked to constrain Gitxaała's use of their traditional territory. Yet utilization remained extensive, and oral history continued to link Gitxaała house groups to the wider ancestral laxyuup irrespective of the colonial legacy.

Experiencing a Gitxaała Social Landscape

The laxyuup of Gitxaała is not simply a physical place. It is a place through which stories and histories pass and are passed along. It is a place that Gitxaała people live within, talk about, use, remember, and long for when they are away. The linkage of place, history, and personal experience was present in the materials Beynon recorded in 1916 and lives today in the oral history of contemporary Gitxaała people.

Gitxaała consider the contemporary village of Lach Klan on Dolphin Island (IR 1, assigned by O'Reilly on September 21, 1882) to be the longest continually inhabited community on the BC coast. Given the depth and extent of the shell midden within the current village this is clearly an ancient site. During a visit in June 2011 our field archaeology research crew conducted an auger test and percussion-coring test adjoining the Church Army building in the center of what was the original village site.[8] A recent construction project had provided a fortuitous opportunity to map and collect a detailed column sample from the surface to bedrock, nearly four meters in depth. The revealed soil profile clearly showed uninterrupted human use and occupancy. Today Lach Klan is the primary village site of Gitxaała, with between 425 and 475 people living there. However, Lach Klan is not the only Gitxaała village site. The oral history recounts many more villages throughout Gitxaała territory.

Other Tsimshianic peoples on the coast deserted their traditional territories and gathered around the Hudson Bay Company fort in the early 1830s and the new Christian missionary community of Metlakatla in 1862. Gitxaała people focused on maintaining access to, use of, and control over their core territory from the base of their long-standing central winter village of Lach Klan.[9]

The villages described in the oral history remain important places socially, culturally, and materially. The following describes specific locations that I have visited or that community members have told me of throughout the course of my life. This is not an exhaustive list of Gitxaała village sites; it does, however, provide a picture of the extent and number of villages that once existed in Gitxaała territory and that remain places of social, cultural, and economic importance today.

The physical experience of being at these places, traveling to them and between them, is a critical aspect of how one comes to know them. Each time I visit a place I find new experiences and paths becoming entangled and woven into my memories and feelings about the place. Traveling along the marine pathways and across the terrestrial trails brings the places alive. It is, as Christopher Tilley (2010, 27) states, "a dialogic relationship between person and landscape."

On the south end of Banks Island, Ks'waan is a large village central to the stories of the encounters with some of the first European visitors (Colnett and his crew). During the course of archaeological research we have determined that this large village site consists of three distinct terraces of houses. In addition analysis of faunal samples show extensive harvesting of abalone and sea urchin at this site.

Ks'waan is a storied place. It is near the harbor, Calamity Bay, where Colnett beached his boats to repair them and replenish his supplies in 1787. It is a place of wonder, situated along the shore of a small cove. The village is tucked just far enough behind a small headland to be perfectly protected from the prevailing southeasterly storms, but it is exposed enough to be able to see anyone coming in to shore. Tall spruce and fir trees outline the back edges of the terraces growing on top of former house posts and rafters.

The first time I stepped ashore there was in the midst of a late spring southeaster. We were drenched by rain. Tim Innes (Ganhada), a member of the boat crew that had brought us here, had described his memories of the place on our trip from Lach Klan. He had last been ashore at Ks'waan as a child sixty years before. He remembered a small trapper's cabin that he had stayed in.

We left the main boat at anchor and ran through the narrow channel between rocks and small islands. Tim had provided detailed directions and a description. It took us twenty minutes to make the journey in our open skiffs through the storm. Standing on the shore it was immediately apparent that we had arrived at a large and ancient village. The village stood about fifteen feet above the high-tide mark. White clamshells could be seen spilling out of the small shore bank that rose to the first terraced platform of the village. We scrambled up the front of the old village and onto the first terrace. The outlines of the old longhouses were plain to see. We saw a second and then a third terrace. We stood quietly listening to the rain pound the undercover. We could see where the posts and beams of the old houses had been from the square lines of two-hundred-year-old spruce and fir trees.

In subsequent years we have returned to systematically collect samples from the surface to the bottom of the anthropogenic soils created by millennia of ancestors who have lived at Ks'waan. In the process we realized that this ancient village has been used continuously for at least five millennia, through the contact period and into the mid-twentieth century.

This place is also special to us for the abalone shells found in the village soils. Abalone is an invertebrate much cherished for food. Its iridescent inner shell is considered a thing of beauty. Yet the dominant scientific discourse has denied us abalone. Report after report claim abalone became a food, a thing of importance to us, only after contact. First it came as a trading good from California on Spanish ships. Then, after the decimation of the sea otter, it was a ubiquitous shoreline creature that we opportunistically started to eat. Yet here at this special place we can see that in fact our ancestors gathered abalone for millennia before the Spanish ever imagined our existence.

Across Principe Channel we find another cluster of villages tucked in behind Wolf Point on the south end of Pitt Island. This place, which has at least five distinct habitation sites, is called Will u sgket. During our archaeological research we identified an intertidal lithic scatter—flaked stones produced in the construction of tools—that included three bifacial points. The lithics recovered were reviewed at UBC and identified as dating to about six thousand years ago. The lithics were found in association with one of the five village sites in this cluster.

Will u sgket is a complex setting, tucked in behind a small island, but with one of the small living sites situated in such a manner that it has a vantage point from which one can see south to Campania Island, to the southwest toward the Estevan Group, and westerly toward Ks'waan. This is a place nestled well out of sight of those passing by. If one doesn't know that there is a small island with a harbor behind it, one would sail on by without suspecting there was more than just another stretch of rain forest. The individual habitation sites at Will u sgket are each smaller than the village at Ks'waan. However, taken together there were as many people here as were living across the way at Ks'waan.

A bit to the east on Pitt Island, in behind the Cherry Islets, is Citeyats (IR 9, established by O'Reilly on July 10, 1891), another large village site. Our archaeological research here has identified the surface features of up to twenty-six house depressions, including at least five large plank houses along the waterfront described by Caamano in his 1792 journal. It is interesting to note that of the reserves established by O'Reilly, only two were primary village sites: Lach Klan and Citeyats. A third, Klapthon (IR 5 and 5A), was proposed as a new primary village closer to the steamship route. The other reserves are all fisheries stations, though at least three have middens or remains of middens within their boundaries. The selection of these fishing stations as reserves reflects the active decisions of Gitxaała chiefs to maintain access to critical fisheries as they ensured a future for their community in the face of increased industrial and colonial encroachment.

The antiquity of this site has been determined by Carbon 14 dating techniques using charcoal samples collected from the deepest portions of the anthropogenic soils. From this we know that Citeyats has been inhabited for at least four thousand years. The archaeological techniques used, systematic grid pattern percussion coring and augering, show clear evidence of continuous human occupation. We can tell this by examining the samples taken from the surface of the village site down to the sterile soil and bedrock, an average of three to four meters below the surface. Careful examination of these samples shows no evidence of breaks in the occupation of this amazing village.

The historical evidence of this village can be found in Caamano's detailed account of his month-long stay while stormbound off the village and his visit ashore as a guest of honor of Gitxaała Sm'ooygit Homstits in 1792. Caamano had a variety of adventures while at anchor, including an occasion on which a number of his crew found themselves stranded, nude on the beach, as the local inhabitants made off with their clothes:

> I had allowed ten of our men to take my galley (the only boat then remaining onboard), for the purpose of landing to wash their clothes, as others had done previously. Half an hour after noon, it was reported to me that one of these hands was seen in the water trying to swim to the ship. I at once ordered a seaman to take a grating and go to his assistance, fearing lest the swimmer should become exhausted. The two men were soon again on board, when I learnt that our washing party had been robbed of the clothes (of which there happened to be a considerable quantity) by natives who had come back to the place where these were, not only in their canoes, but along the shore as well. The Indians were numerous and carried weapons. Our people, alarmed by this, offered no resistance, but thought only to save their lives by flight. Some fled into the forest, others threw themselves on to logs in the water, in an endeavour to reach the ship as the natives had seized the galley and carried off the two boats' keepers. (Wagner and Newcombe 1938, 276–77)

The crew did eventually get their clothing back, and Caamano received an invitation to a feast in one of the longhouses in the village of Citeyats.

People lived at Citeyats well into the twentieth century. At some point in the mid-1800s occupation shifted from year-round to seasonal. Just to the north of the main village site are the remains of a small trapping cabin. People still continue to visit the old village. Small trails lead from a house platform near the beach, used to pitch a tent on, through patches of *wooms*, *waakyil*, and *wiiłeexs* (harvestable shrubs and berries).

Farther up the shore, in Twartz Inlet, a commercial drag seine was operated from the late nineteenth to the mid-twentieth century. Farther to the east, in Union Pass, is another drag seine camp that operated over the same period of time. Both of these camps were located on reserves that Ts'ibasaa had set up in meetings with O'Reilly in 1891 and were Gitxaała sockeye fishing sites. While people no longer use these places to fish salmon as they did in the previous century, community members still find the time to visit.

To the south of Citeyats on Campania Island and within the Estevan Group are more Gitxaała villages and places of social and cultural significance. Old villages, like Citeyats and Ks'waan, stand along the shore of Campania and on the exposed coastline of the Estevan Group. To the south Gitxaała people have used habitation sites on Moore Islands during their customary harvesting of fish, seals, and other marine resources. These are tough places to get to, being on the extreme edge of the interface between land and ocean. Locations like these are why Gitxaała people say we are people of the saltwater, for not only is the majority of our food gathered from the ocean, but Gitxaała live so close to the ocean as to be essentially a part of the ocean itself.

The skipper Charles Bishop recorded meeting with Gitxaała people in Waller Bay on the rugged exposed west coast of Banks Island in 1795:

> The first place we came to was the butchery, where lay about 40 dead Seals, newly killed. Ten or 12 more, was on the Fire, Singing the Hair off the Skins. A Women and a man where Stripping the blubber and Skin together, off an other Quantity. Another women was cutting up and Quartering the Flesh. Many Poles spread from tree to tree about 6 feet over the Fire where Covered with Strips of Blubber, and on bushes all round was hung the Flesh. Blood Gutts and filth formed the comfortable foot Path to the Habitation which lay about 10 yards from the butchery. This was no other than some Poles stretched from tree to tree about 7 feet from the Ground and covered with the Rind of the Birch Tree. A large fire right in the middle served as well to warm the inhabitants as to dry their Fish, vast quantities of which were hung to the Poles and spread around the Rocks near the Hutt: This Family consisted of an old man, 3 of middle age and two young ones, and they had

Each a Wife seemingly Proportioned to their own ages, which with 4 small Children composed the group. (Roe 1967, 65)

To the north of Waller Bay our archaeological research has recorded information on three habitation sites in Kxenk'aa'wen (Bonilla Arm). All are sites that have been used from the ancient past (more than two thousand years) to the contemporary period. As described in chapter 8, this is also the site of an impressive complex of stone fish traps that extends for more than a kilometer along the shore.

To the east of Banks Island in Ktsm laagn (Curtis Inlet) is the village established by Ts'ibasaa when he first chose his domains within Gitxaała territory. This village was established long before the flood mentioned in the ancient oral histories.

When Ts'ibassa and his Gispuwada group came down the Skeena from Temlaxham they went to where there were already some of the Laxskik group in Lach Klan. This was a gathering place where these people had their elevation feasts. . . . Bu Ts'ibassa wanted to have his own exclusive hunting territories so he set out, to find an exclusive place for himself and his own family (matrilineal). He found a long inlet and called it Kts'ml'aa'agn (crevice in mountain). The entrance to this inlet being very narrow and between two high bluffs gave it an appearance of being a crevice in a rock. (Beynon notebook, 1916, BF 421.29, CMC)

In 1916 Beynon recorded the names of houses that Ts'ibasaa and his brothers built at Ktsm laagn: "In Kts'ml'aa'agn, the hunting ground of He:l (Ts'ibassa), he had also the following houses mijom welp. Shower House. Mik̲—shower of rain. The front of this house was decorated as having a shower of rain in front of it by painting. This was used by all of the house of He:l. Maxaiam welp. Rainbow house. This was built by Niaswexs at Kts'ml'aa'agn and was used by all the royal family" (Beynon notebook, 1916, BF 421.29, CMC).

Beynon describes all of the various houses that Ts'ibasaa had throughout his territories, but these two are of special relevance given their location at Ts'ibasaa's first home within the Gitxaała laxyuup. During several trips to Ktsm laagn I have had the opportunity to stand on the house platforms that remain from the ancient village site. They have a clear view of the seaward approach and allow for effective control over entry to the inlet. At the head of the inlet and by the sockeye salmon stream are the remains of several twentieth-century cabins used during the drag seine period.

Our archaeological research has described a small village site and a remnant midden patch of some antiquity. The faunal analysis of the site shows a heavy reliance on salmon and herring. This place remains a significant cultural location and resource-harvesting location.

K'moda (Lowe Inlet) is on the mainland shore of Grenville Channel but is also directly accessible from Ktsm laagn if one were to follow the sockeye stream and lake system located at the head of the inlet. K'moda is one of the central cultural places within the Gitxaała laxyuup. This is where the contemporary reserves were negotiated, but, more important, this place marks the most southerly advance of northern invaders, who were eventually repulsed by the Gitxaała. It is a key fishing site for the royal Gispuwada house of Ts'ibasaa-He:l and an ancient village that figures prominently in Gitxaała adaawx (Menzies and Butler 2007).

As I explain in chapters 4 and 8, K'moda figures prominently in my own family history and personal experiences. It is a place I visited many times with family members heading south to fish in the waters near Citeyats, walking along the shores and trails on family trips, and more recently as a researcher mapping the ancient village and collecting soil samples to analyze for faunal remains as part of a larger project reconstructing ancient Gitxaała harvesting practices.

All of these places exist in several temporal frames. They are ancient sites ranging back in time from two to nearly ten millennia. Each has a local history that is linked to named hereditary leaders and real individuals who spent their lives connected to these places. These are contemporary places that Gitxaała people visit and know through direct experience, memories, and stories. But these places also exist in an abstract frame, almost out of time, as markers of social relations that, while rooted in history, have direct meaning in the present.

Home

Ultimately one experiences the laxyuup directly and personally. It can be described, as I have attempted to do, in terms of its geographical extent. One can discuss the ways colonialism has constrained and infringed upon Gitxaała practices and activities within the laxyuup. The real meaning and experience of this place for Gitxaała people comes from time spent on the water and land that form the laxyuup, listening to the sounds of the place and the stories of our history told while one is within and upon it. This is the experience of coming home.

~~~~

4

~~~~

Adaawx

History and the Past

History is integral to Gitxaała identity. There is little about Gitxaała
that is not touched by historical references. In this chapter I focus on
the documentation of Gitxaała oral history. I do so in two steps: (1) I
outline a general theory of history drawing from my knowledge and
research within and on behalf of Gitxaała Nation, and (2) I offer three
stories of oral history research that exemplify a Gitxaała approach to
the documentation of oral history.

A Theory of History

This general theory of history draws from the intersection of my own
personal history and my professional practice. I grew up hearing about
my family history as a normal practice of everyday life. As a professional anthropologist I have been asked by the political leadership of
Gitxaała, over the course of more than a decade, to provide expert
opinions on the existence of Gitxaała as a people with a distinct history, culture, and system of governance. Since 1998 I have observed
and participated in a wide array of feasts, community meetings, inter-
community meetings, and public meetings as a professional anthropologist. During these events Gitxaała people would, in the normal
course of their interventions and contributions, make statements about
the importance of their history and how it ought to be relayed. Public
statements reference historical processes and events, acknowledge
those present who have connections to the history, and then recount

the particular history or acknowledge that the history heard was in fact consistent with what they had been taught by their own elders.

In the course of conducting field research with Gitxaała people related to traditional territories and their use I was regularly advised that the appropriate approach to research involved requesting permission of the named title holder to the territory in question and that any conversation with community members should include groups of people who held the rights to tell the history. The emphasis was that even in direct communications, such as interviews and conversations, the transmission of history and related information needed to take place in a collective setting with appropriate individuals in place to acknowledge and witness what was being said.

In conversations with my mentors I have had the opportunity to discuss and learn about the ways knowledge is transmitted. In these settings, which parallel traditional approaches to the transmission of knowledge, I have learned about the processes of learning. This involves the learner listening, not questioning, observing and then doing. Knowledge about history is transmitted in these settings through direct instruction, demonstration, and practice.

Documentary sources also provide corroborating information on oral history and its transmission. William Beynon recorded a great many historical narratives; throughout his work can be found comments and asides related to the nature of Tsimshian oral history and the ways it can or should be related. In his 1916 notebooks of observations of and interviews collected in the village of Lach Klan, for example, Beynon records that his entire research project was placed on hold until the leading hereditary leader, Joshua Tsibassa, granted approval.

> The people have not advanced as much as the other people of other tribes in matters of education and still adhere to ancient ceremonies. I had difficulty in getting started here on account of this and on going to an informant to get information in the house of Tsybɛsɣ I saw the informant [Sam Lewis, who then] took me to the house of the chief and asked the necessary permission to be able to give me the information and after I had paid him for

his work, he handed all the money over to the chief and took only what the chief allowed him for telling me what I wanted. (Beynon notebook, 1916, vol. 1, BF 419, box 29, CMC)

Then, midway through his research, a number of Beynon's respondents withdrew their participation; they were waiting for further permission to be granted by hereditary leaders to answer Beynon's additional questions.

My informant upon being requested to translate other names refused to do so until she had received the consent of the different chiefs. . . .

Informant for the house of 'nagap't, ganhada. Mary 'Ałaxsgɛ̀ls 75 yrs of age. (Beynon notebook, 1916, vol. 1, BF 419, box 29, CMC)

This process of ensuring approval, proceeding, stopping, and reaffirming approval is a long-standing practice among Gitxaała people. It is part of the internal mechanisms and protocols that ensure the maintenance and continuity of an oral history over time.

Oral history, in a Gitxaała sense, is usually referred to as adaawx, lineage histories or "true tellings." These narratives relate the origin and central events of a lineage. Adaawx revolve around named hereditary leaders whose names are passed down through time. Adaawx reference places, events, people, privileges (crests, songs, stories, etc.), things (tangible and intangible) that form property, and rights within Gitxaała society. Adaawx also contain references to traditions and laws that govern social behavior and the relations between humans and between humans and all other social beings (animals, spirits, etc.).

The authority to relate these narratives rests in the idea of *malsk* (literally, "telling"). The emphasis here is on the act of relating, the act of telling. The authority to tell arises from an encounter with *naxnox* (loosely translated as "supernatural being" or "supernatural") wherein certain rights, privileges, or property are granted to the named hereditary leader who is the protagonist of the history. Malsk signifies ownership and thus the right to tell certain stories. It provides the authority to named hereditary leaders and in so doing mirrors the structure of authority and hierarchy that resides among the na̲xnox—which is the ultimate source of authority and power.

History and tradition are linked through the idea and concept of *ɫagyigyet,* which literally means "old people" or "people of the long ago and tradition." This is important as it highlights that tradition is integral to the Gitxaała notion of history. Embedded in the telling of history are ideas (values, principles, practices) that instruct people on how to behave in the contemporary world. Thus ideas related to resource management and sharing, for example, are directly embedded in the telling and learning of Gitxaała history.

The transmission of oral narratives occurs in a range of settings, including but not limited to formal settings such as feasts and training or instruction of heirs and youth.

Transmission of History in Formal Settings

The feast system is the primary formal setting within which oral narratives are recounted. Margaret Anderson and Marjorie Halpin (2000) edited Beynon's 1945 notebooks that detail the proceedings of a multiday traditional Tsimshian feast. The Spanish skipper J. Caamano provides one of the earliest European recordings of a feast during his visit to Gitxaała territory in 1792 (Wagner and Newcombe 1938). Both accounts describe similar processes wherein leading hereditary leaders and hosts relate their lineage histories through song and dance, and both describe how these tellings are witnessed by the observing hereditary leaders.

The importance of public witnessing of events in this formal setting is great. Among the Gitxaała to stand up and acknowledge a history is to agree with it; public disagreement takes the form of silence. This differs from Euro-American traditions of dissent. Drawing upon work by Margaret Seguin (1984), Anderson and Halpin (2000, 34) have this to say about silence as an expression of disagreement:

> Silence indicates that you are in disagreement with what has been said, and on a situation of any importance the speaker will rephrase in order to elicit an overt expression of agreement. This is

precisely the strategy that was followed by "older thought" at Gitsegukla [an inland Skeena River Tsimshianic community] when they disagreed with the plans of the "younger thought" with regard to a modernized style for the pole-raising and concomitant ceremonies. They not only showed their disagreement by their silence, but two of them moved out of the community, which was correctly read by the "younger thought" as a strong and compelling message.

Non-Indigenous observers often overlook the role of silence as an act of dissent and disagreement. Within the Euro-American cultural tradition silence is seen as passive acceptance or lack of knowledge related to a subject under discussion. However, within Gitxaała and related Tsimshian groups, silence is an active form of disagreement and is understood as such. This has several serious implications in the context of contemporary research.

Research that is not supported by hereditary leaders or community members may not be overtly opposed. Rather community members who are knowledgeable may simply exempt themselves from the process by their absence (not being home when the researcher knocks, missing prearranged appointments, leaving the community to go fishing, etc.). Or, if these same members are approached directly by a researcher they may politely demur and say they don't really know much about the subject. Unfortunately an inexperienced researcher may conclude from this that there is no objection to his or her work and that few people know much about the subject of the research.

Gitxaała oral accounts are replete with stories of visiting twentieth-century researchers who came, visited matriarchs and house leaders, sipped tea and ate cookies, and then left with none of the real history. Yet these same researchers often go on to write and publish accounts in which they profess expertise, even when the knowledge they sought was withheld from them. From within the Gitxaała frame of reference these researchers reveal their ineptitude (even when external agencies, such as governments or university publishers, accept at face value the inept researcher's findings).

In order for formal transmission of narratives to occur there needs be an opportunity for community members to learn their history. Those who are in line to inherit hereditary names are expected to learn their history as part of the process of taking on their name; in addition all members of a house are also expected to learn the general history of their lineage. As this is a ranked society there are aspects of history and tradition that are restricted, not only according to house group but also according to one's rank and position within a house group. The training of those in line to inherit takes place in all manner of contexts, including but not limited to home, work, play, harvesting and processing foods and materials, learning dances and songs within the family and (in current times), and local dance and drum groups.

Three Stories of Oral History Research

These three stories illuminate a Gitxaała approach to the documentation of oral history, but they do so from three rather different aspects. The first two are examples mandated and requested by Gitxaała Nation leadership in the context of documenting community use and occupancy over a disputed area of Prince Rupert Harbor. Here the task was to document knowledge related to places in response to a specific contemporary legal dispute. Though linked to each other by a shared purpose, these are stories of two different approaches to telling history and reflect differences in the gendered telling of history. Thus in one location matriarchs spoke and engaged (around the table), but in the other it was the smgigyet and *lik'agyet* (councilors) who participated and who were the primary speakers. More than gender, though, these two stories of oral history research also document a trajectory of learning with the researcher cast in the role of learner. That is, a shift from sitting around a table—it could be a coffee table, a kitchen table, or, as in this case, a classroom table—to traveling through and to the places that one heard about when sitting around the table. This is similar to the way place-based knowledge is typically transmitted intergenerationally within Gitxaała. This approach to teaching history is brought into closer focus by the third story, about my trips to K'moda with family and in my capacity as a professional researcher. Here my personal and professional interests are entwined as I traveled with family to learn more about a place that I have grown up hearing about and have visited many times.

Under Canadian law aboriginal communities have to demonstrate that they have used and have occupied the lands they claim title to and claim they have rights to. An entire industry has been built up to document use and occupancy that includes an abundance of technical consultants and lawyers. The situation has been complicated by the process of colonial displacement, such as the rise of missionary communities like William Duncan's Metlakatla, postcontact fur trading villages like Port Simpson, and industrial centers like Klemtu, each of which has played a role in restructuring Indigenous memories of place and belonging. For communities like Gitxaała that have retained a direct connection to their traditional laxyuup, this is a doubly perplexing matter, as they are defending their territory not only against the Canadian state but also against those Indigenous neighbors who have turned away from the customary laws and have adopted a more Eurocentric approach to land and land rights. The first two stories of oral history arose from the need to identify and defend the laxyuup Gitxaała.

Place-Names Workshop

About twenty hereditary leaders and matriarchs have gathered in a classroom at the local college in Prince Rupert. I've prepared the room by placing the tables together in the center with chairs circling them. On the wall at the front of the class I have taped up a marine chart of Gitxaała laxyuup. Post-it notes and felt pens are ready on the table. To the side of the room is a coffee pot and baked goods from the local bakery. Everyone is talking—sounds of English and sm'algyax intermingle. I don't speak sm'algyax (we have interpreters ready to help me), but I do recognize some words and phrases. Most of the older folks, those sixty or more, are more comfortable speaking in sm'algyax. More critically, the information most important to the discussion is spoken in sm'algyax to ensure precision in what is said and recorded. After the meeting the audio tapes are transcribed, translated, and checked against my own notes of the meeting and the recollections of key participants.

What follows is a condensed version of the workshop that highlights a series of important narrative threads, encounters, and lessons. As Walter Benjamin (1969, 86) explains, every real story "contains, openly or covertly, something useful. The usefulness may, in one case, consist of a moral; in another, in some practical advice; in a third, in a proverb or maxim. In every case the storyteller is a man [in this case, also a woman] who has counsel for his readers [in the oral context—listeners]. . . . Counsel is less an answer to a question than a proposal concerning the continuation of a story which is just unfolding." Those versed in modern reports and direct question-and-answer modes will be frustrated by what they hear. The narrative seems to shift, jump, return to the start, and then get deflected yet again. Benjamin writes, "The storyteller takes what he tells from experience—his own or that reported by others. And he in turn makes it the experience of those who are listening to his tale" (87). The stories told to me during this workshop drew from the gathered experience of those present and were told so as to instruct me in my task.

I opened the meeting by pointing to the charts: "We are looking at some charts on the wall from Banks Island up to Prince Rupert. I am looking for direction: a place to start, a place and time to link Gitxaała history to events, people, names within the laxyuup."

Laxgibu sigyidm hana'a Janet Moody responds in sm'algyax (words spoken in English at this meeting are italicized), "We go back before the flood. To the old people [łagyigyet]. That's what the old people called it at the time of the flood—shla giget. There's one thing that I heard where our people anchored [during the flood]. One place where our old people anchored. *Oona River*, but it wasn't called *Oona River* then. That's another place where they anchored—*Oona River*: Kwi nax. I have also heard that *Metlakatla* was originally Maach le Git xaala. I heard that too. That's why it's called *Metlakatla*."

Pointing to Prince Rupert on the marine chart, she says, "Tk'aan: *Prince Rupert*. There is a story for this. The white people couldn't translate it. That's why they call it *Kaien Island*.

"I want to call Samson to tell a story of another village, about this supernatural [naxnox] creature that came up in this one area. *Seal Cove*—I want you to show it to them. *Sourdough Bay*. The white man called it that. And he called it Wiil Luu Gyeben. A place where the supernatural creature comes up."

SAMSON COLLINSON (GANHADA): Maach le . . . What did they call this place? There's one place through that pass—Maachle Sh'bee'shk'n. I think that's what they call it. [This is a different place they are referring to now.] There's an opening there, another channel.

JANET: What this Sh'bee'shk'n mean? Is it numbers?

RITA ROBINSON (GISPUWADA): Yes, Sh'bee'shk'n da' goh'opsken? How many is that?

RICHARD SPENCER (GANHADA): *Ten* [Sh'bee'shk'n means "ten"]. The only time you use this word is when you count trees. One, two, three, and so forth. So you only use this set of numbers for counting trees.

MATTHEW HILL (Laskiik): This is my comment of what I heard Mason Brown say: "When we built a bird trap" [hap'ch jo'och. Everyone giggles; "bird trap" is a double entendre].

The sighamana sing the bird trap song.

Ch'een juoth. Ch'een nawaaps nayanth. [Come in bird, come in bird, come into your grandfather's house.]

The song ends. Following a moment of cheerful silence Samson starts to talk quietly from his seat near the back of the room: "A small island. This island, where they hunt big deer on top of this mountain. And our people went up there to hunt for them. That's what my uncle Joseph Shaw told me. My uncle said he had been able to walk up there too. [He was likely fairly old by that time.] On top of this mountain on this island, with all these big deer. These deer have short legs. This island— that's where there was a sea lion with no teeth, on that island. That's why they called it Lhaach kasch waan [literally, 'The place of no teeth']."

While Samson speaks Rita turns to Janet: "Isn't that the place where this humpback whale drifted ashore there, on that island? And this whale had no teeth? Do you remember?"

SAMSON: Those people [ɬagyigyet] knew the signs before the oolichan would come to the Nass. This is what I don't know. I don't know specifically what sign they were looking at. How they knew when these oolichan were coming through there.

RICHARD: What is the name of that bird, when they first come out?

UNIDENTIFIED: Sh'oh [robin]?

RICHARD: No, not that one.

UNIDENTIFIED: Le'eds [grouse].

RICHARD: When the grouse first comes, when they first heard the grouse, that's the first sign that the oolichans are coming. And that's when these oolichans came to Kl'ooh'xsm's [Nass River]. And that's a sign. When these grouse—when they hear them, that's the sign.

RITA: Violet told, there is a tunnel somewhere by Oona River. And that's where the oolichans go through, through this tunnel. And those oolichans, they're the ones that go to Skeena River. And that's why you see all these seagulls around that area, that's where the oolichans go through the tunnel to go to Skeena. That's what Violet told me. Did you hear about that as well, Matt?

MATTHEW: Yes, I've heard. It was just like silver in that area in the water.

LARRY BOLTON (GISPUWADA): There's one place my dad showed me where we fished. Where my dad told me that our people lived there. It was called Tshl'oh (Slide). What did those white people call that cannery?

UNIDENTIFIED: Inverness.

MATTHEW: My heart is getting stronger for what I am hearing today. Ever since this issue came about. These white people had nothing to do about this port. And the government broke a lot of their own laws. So they can get what they want, it's only money that they are looking at. They really don't care about our territory. And what's been coming out today, the world is going to see it. We could show it to them so that they will step back. They do not follow our laws and they did not consult us.

They should have consulted us in the first place. And that's why this man [Charles Menzies] is trying to help us and to show us the right direction to head to. I see that Charles was uplifted for all the knowledge sharing that has happened. This man here is trying to get us ready for where we're at today. I can see that Charles was very uplifted when he started hearing all the adaawx [oral histories] that he heard from these people. And also in this harbor here. It's been two years that Charles has been trying to help us [with the port issue]. We have gone quite a ways now. . . . My heart is happy that he's seen what is happening now. For the discussions that we are making about this port now, that's what I want to say. That's what I want to say to Charles. [Says as an aside:] That's what the old people would call him—Chaales. [Everyone laughs].

Robins, double entendres, oolichans and underground tunnels, mountaintops, hunting, old people, and the topic at hand—the Prince Rupert harbor and port: the workshop covered a lot of ground. These may appear disconnected points. They clearly are not direct and explicit answers to the question of who owns Prince Rupert Harbor. They are, however, examples of the living history of Gitxaała and the many interconnections that link people, place, and history in a woven blanket that lies upon laxyuup Gitxaała.

Naming the Harbor

It's an early May morning in Prince Rupert Harbor. The sky is clear blue and the air is crisp. The *Katrena Leslie*, the Gitxaała Nation's sixty-foot fishing boat, is tied to the dock, its engine running, waiting for the day's work. Our task, documented in the film *Naming the Harbour*, is to take a group of Gitxaała hereditary leaders on a tour of the harbor and to record their stories, memories, and histories of this place.

As the boat pulls away from the dock Deputy Chief Clarence Innis, a Gispuwada sm'ooygit, explains the purpose of the trip. I'm here to write down what is said and later to prepare a written report. Ernie Bolton, a community interpreter, Jen Rashleigh, a filmmaker, and my son Tristan, who is taking photographs, join me in this task.

Clarence introduces the team to the hereditary leaders. He describes the intended outcomes: a film, a report, and a photo essay. After he's done Ernie repeats everything in sm'algy<u>a</u>x to ensure that everyone has understood.

We're all squeezed into the boat's galley. Some folks are seated around the galley table. The younger people stand, pressed close to the table. We're looking at a marine chart of the harbor.

Richard Spencer points to a place: "Kloya. That is named after a type of berry. There's crab apples there. It's a sockeye creek. This is a place Gitxaała people have lived. Kennedy Island, this is another important place. I have a huge story to tell, an adaawx that lies on that place. A story from way back, a story from the time of the old people."

Alan Brown (Laskiik) says, "Nathan Shaw,[1] he was a passenger on our boat. He would tell us about places along our way from the village to Prince Rupert." Alan is pointing to places on the map as he describes them. Others nod their heads. Occasionally people will murmur agreement. Everyone is listening carefully as Alan continues.

"Y'asim [Grandfather] Nathan spoke about the Kinahan Islands [near the mouth of Prince Rupert Harbor]. There was a village there. There were fish traps for ground fish. Also, at the mouth of Delusion Bay there is a fish trap there. There is an inlet on Smith Island that has spring salmon traps. Casey Point. The shape of the shoreline was changed by Gitxaała people. This is right by the port. [The site has now been completely destroyed by the port's expansion.]"

Richard adds, "Behind Casey Point, this is where the port is expanding. When they dig back they will find artifacts. They will flatten this. Our history lives there."

Alan agrees. "Y'asim Nathan told me the same story. There were so many wars. On the sand bar that was there [he points toward Casey Point on the map] the old people made a false village. When the warriors came, when the Haida came, they saw the houses there. On top of the mountain the Gitxaała had built a structure of logs and gravel and sand. It was a weapon. When the Haida came ashore to raid the false village the Gitxaała released the logs and the side of the mountain came down and buried the Haida warriors. Telling the story on the spot. Telling adaawx on the spot. It brings the memories back."

Alan, Richard, and the others continue in this vein as the boat heads out of the harbor. When we come up to Coast Island, outside Prince Rupert Harbor and just off the industrial port on Ridley Island, the boat is slowed to a stop. Everyone goes out on deck. Richard begins to tell the story of two young Gitxaała children, guardians of a special treasure, who had been kidnapped by the Haida: "The Haida attacked a Gitxaała family that were living in Porpoise Harbor. The brother and sister had been trained by their family so that they would know what to do if they were attacked. The people were from Guniałwz [Moore Island, a place to the far south of Gitxaała territory]. This was the same family. It is where the story lives. The Haida people knew that these people had a treasure. The family had a feeling that sooner or later warriors were going to come. They instructed the children—to make sure the treasure was safe—they showed them where the treasure was and gave them instructions as what to do if the family was attacked."

The boat is drifting just inside of Coast Island, incidentally the site of a planned deep-sea loading dock that will go right over this culturally significant place and obliterate it. As Richard talks he points to places in the water, on the island, back toward the harbor: he is illustrating his story. People nod their heads and murmur agreement in English and sm'algyax as Richard continues.

"The boy and girl were taken captive by the Haida. Right here, close to this rock here. Mason Brown [a late elder and hereditary leader] told this. Inside this rock they dropped the bag. The story goes on. I can stand here and say this place belongs to Gitxaała. We didn't just move here one hundred seventy-five years ago.[2] We've been here before the flood."

MATTHEW HILL: I have heard this story. Our family had a boat, *Quitonksa*, we transported people. Our elders always shared stories along the way. What we hear today I have heard many times before on my family's boat.

SAM LEWIS (GANHADA): I'm so grateful I'm here today. What Richard is saying, I too have heard a lot of stories. People used to row. They camped on the way as they traveled through our territory. We have places up and down the coast.

LARRY BOLTON: [speaking in sm'algyax̲] I too have heard these stories. Thank you chiefs, matriarchs, for being here.

Everyone on board took a moment to speak, to acknowledge what they had heard, and to add their own account of Gitxaała's history of use and occupancy in and around Prince Rupert's harbor. While the setting—the deck of a commercial fishing boat—was novel, the context of place-based storytelling has a long history with Gitxaała and other Indigenous societies (Basso 1996). As I go on to discuss, stories—histories—of lineages and community are told and taught in a variety of places, and one of the most important times for telling is while at the place or places that factor strongly in the story.

Traveling to K'moda

Going to K'moda in March 2001 was both a personal and a professional trip. Unlike in the first two oral histories, this trip was motivated by my desire to learn more about my own family's history. Joining me on this trip was my father, Basso Menzies, my uncle Russell Gamble and cousin Teddy Gamble; my two sons; and my colleague Caroline Butler. This would not be the first time I had visited K'moda. While working with my father on his commercial fishing boat for three decades we had stopped here en route to the south or north countless times. This is a storied place for me. I grew up hearing stories about my great-grandfather Edward Gamble and his life and connections to this place. What made this particular trip special was being able to go there in the company of sm'ooygit H:el, Russell Gamble, and other members of my family. It was thus an opportunity to learn through direct participation and observation.

Understanding the importance of place is critical in comprehending history. In each of these examples the places become something more than merely a setting, though they are of course a setting within and against which people have lived, worked, played, and currently engage in the context of struggles to assert aboriginal rights and title. However, these places take on a presence of their own that fundamentally structures, shapes, and even enables human telling of events. These places are mnemonic devices, memory aids, spurs to reminiscences, and actors in history and memories in their own right. It is as though these places have a form of agency in the telling and revealing of their own histories.

The trip to K'moda began for earnest when I stepped onto the dock at Lach Klan and was greeted by Teddy and Russell. My sons, my father, my research colleague, and I had flown out from Prince Rupert by float plane; we were now going to run south on Teddy's thirty-eight-foot fishing boat, the *Gamble Lake* (named for the large lake that feeds K'moda). We loaded our gear onto the boat, let go the lines, and headed toward K'moda. On the way down my father and Russell spoke about their lives fishing and what they each remembered about K'moda. Teddy ran the boat, and I watched my two young boys. We sat quietly, for the most part, listening in on the galley conversation. Caroline would occasionally ask a question, but mostly the two older men did the talking. As we drew nearer to K'moda the conversation began to wane as all eagerly turned toward what lay ahead.

We dropped anchor, set up the small skiff we were using to run ashore, and then we were there! The tide was dropping as we landed on the shore. We pulled the skiff up on a cleared patch of the beach, what archaeologists call a canoe skid.

"This is where we hauled the drag seine skiff up," Russell said as we piled out of the skiff onto the beach. "It should be up there." He pointed toward the trees a few dozen feet away. My sons took off in that direction. It didn't take long for them to find the remains of the old boat.

On the beach Russell began to describe the way the place looked when he actively worked the drag seine in the middle years of the twentieth century. "There were two houses up there. Beside this big rock we had a clothesline." He looked around. "I think the ground's washed away here. I don't think the rocks were out like this."

As we stood there listening and watching, Russell turned toward the large half-moon-shaped fish trap. "See the hole there, where the rocks are knocked away? That's where the DFO [Department of Fisheries and Oceans] knocked the wall down. They said it was killing fish."

As the tide dropped, Russell, my father, and Teddy started to talk about salmon fishing. Caroline and I measured and roughly mapped in the size and shape of the stone trap. My boys ran back and forth across the beach, as young children are wont to do; their voices were layered over the lower tones of my uncle, father, and cousin.

Since 2001 I have returned several times to K'moda with Teddy as part of a Gitxaała-led archaeological research project. Our primary focus has been to document the nature and extent of the stone fish trap (Menzies 2012; Menzies and Butler 2007; Smethurst 2014). Our crew has been university students and community members.

Each visit brings a new and deeper sense of the place. At the core of our learning is a twining of the oral history—both of lineage and of the more recent past—with a growing understanding of the material evidence of my family's history in this place. Each subsequent trip has found something more as we learn things that reverberate with the oral history of K'moda.

From the fish trap to the mid-twentieth-century houses we have started to learn about the ancient village site that is part of this place. From the shoreline adjacent to the fish trap we have cast our gaze farther out and have seen more traps and stone alignments. It is as though the conversation we began that cold bright day in March a decade or so ago continues as we grow in our knowledge of K'moda.

Summary

There are two phrases that I think best expresses the Gitxaała idea of history: "History lives there" and "A story lies over this place." In each of the examples of oral history research we heard variations of these two phrases. At the place-names workshop each place was linked to a story, a person who told the story, and an event or character that figured prominently in the story. None of the places discussed existed abstracted from history; it was the histories or stories that in fact gave the places meaning and importance. On the boat trip the speakers explicitly spoke of stories living in particular areas and of the stories lying upon the physical landscape very much in the way a blanket is laid upon a person at a feast. There is weight to these stories; they lie upon the physical and social landscapes; they have consequence beyond the simple moment of their telling. The act of visiting K'moda time and time again brings forth new memories and understandings. Being in a place also brings forth memories of the stories.

Stories—more properly adaawx and malsk—lie upon and live in places. These stories, like the people telling them and like the beings the stories are about, are in and of themselves a type of living entity. These stories are understood to exist in some sense independently of people, yet they simultaneously rely upon people to tell and teach them.

Gitxaała's conception of history has important consequences for research. First, it suggests that histories of relevance to place are best told in particular contexts. Second, the learning and comprehension of these stories occur over long periods of time. Third, learners need to be ready and open to hear the stories and to present themselves with patience.

These opening four chapters lay out the foundation of being Gitxaała: names, governance, place, and history. These four dimensions of social and political relations define a cultural framework and set of principles for being Gitxaała. As we move forward in this story we encounter the material processes of production and the social relations of food production. Here the cultural practices of being Gitxaała are enacted in the harvesting and processing of Gitxaała's own foods.

Fig. 1. (*top*) Visiting K'moda with (*left to right*) one of the author's sons, Sm'ooygit He:l (Russell Gamble), Marvin "Teddy" Gamble, and Basso Menzies, March 2001.

Fig. 2. (*bottom*) A tour of Prince Rupert Harbor with Gitxaała hereditary leadership, May 2008.

Fig. 3. (*above*) A chart showing Gitxaała places and histories in the area of Prince Rupert Harbor, January 2008.

Fig. 4. (*opposite top*) *Left to right*: Russell Gamble, Jon Irons, and Naomi Smethurst excavating a hearth at Ks'waan, June 2011.

Fig. 5. (*opposite bottom*) The author cleaning fish onboard Marvin "Teddy" Gamble's gillnetter, the *Gamble Lake*, July 2012.

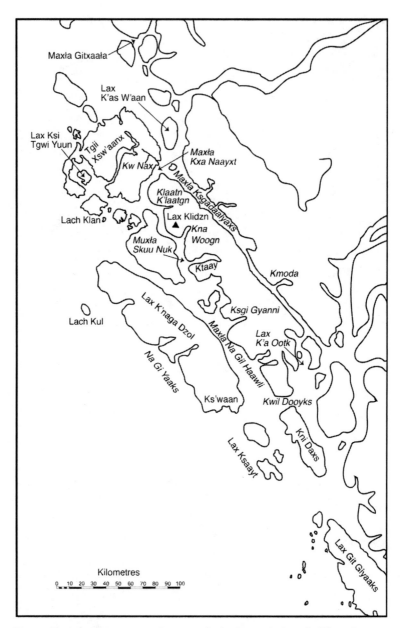

Map 1. Gitxaała place-names. Cartography by Kenneth Campbell based on information provided by the author.

Maxła Gitxaała

Lax K'as W'aan

Lax Ksi Tgwi Yuun

Tgii Xsw'aanx

Maxła Kxa Naayxt

Kw Nax

Maxła Ksgadaalyaxs

Klaatn K'laatgn

Lax Klidzn

Lach Klan

Kna Woogn

Muxła Skuu Nuk

Ktaay

Kmoda

Lach Kul

Lax K'naga Dzol

Ksgi Gyanni

Lax K'a Ootk

Na Gii Yaaks

Maxła Na Gii Haawli

Ks'waan

Kwil Dooyks

Kni Daxs

Lax Ksaayt

Lax Git Giyaaks

Kilometres

0 10 20 30 40 50 60 70 80 90 100

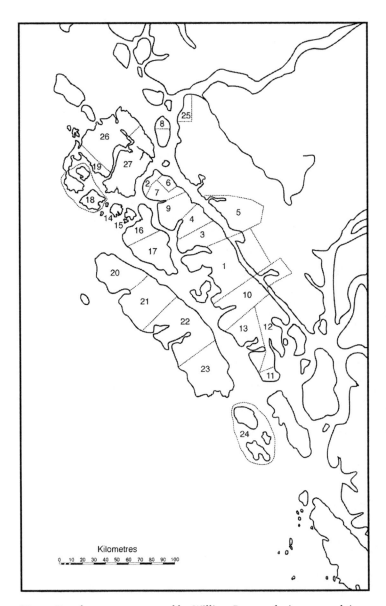

Map 2. Based on a map prepared by William Beynon during research in Lach Klan, 1916. The map is not an accurate reflection of laxyuup Gitxaała, as Beynon did not personally survey or visit the places described on the map, nor was he at that time familiar with the actual territory itself. Numbers refer to hunting territories described by Beynon and discussed in the text. Cartography by Kenneth Campbell.

5

Sihoon

Catching Fish

Gitxaała are a marine people. Though mountains and valleys are important, fish and fishing is what defines the core of being Gitxaała. Whether one is catching fish, cooking fish, sharing fish, or eating fish, the Gitxaała world revolves around the marine places and practices that provide a phenomenally rich and abundant source of marine foods. "These are gourmet foods," Matthew Hill said at a 2008 feast in Lach Klan. "Anywhere else these are gourmet foods. In Gitxaała these are everyday foods." Community members fully understand the global importance and value placed on Gitxaała's food.

This chapter provides an overview of the social and economic importance of marine fisheries for Gitxaała. First I consider the doctrine of respect that guides Gitxaała fisheries. Next I consider the thousands of years of resource harvesting and the crucial role of trade and exchange of marine resources, and finally I review of the transformation of Gitxaała fisheries since the arrival of Ḵ'amksiwa̱h. This chapter is followed by three separate accounts of marine resources that hold a special place in Gitxaała's world: herring and herring roe, abalone, and salmon.

Respect and Gitxaała Fisheries

Gitxaała fisheries, as cultural practices, are framed in terms of relations between social beings. That is, one's behavior is regulated through social relations, which are understood as kin-like (see, for example, Langdon 2006), with the animals one harvests and the people one harvests with. This implies and requires a structure of obligation and reciprocity. One learns this firsthand through experience on the water and land. But these lessons are also heard and reinforced in the oral histories of Gitxaała people, some of which have been recorded over the past century and a half.

John Tait (Gispaxloats, Tsimshian) recounted a sequence of stories of Txemsum (Raven) to William Beynon in 1954. In his narrative Tait talks about the time Txemsum married the princess of the Salmon People. Txemsum "had plenty of food. Whenever they were hungry they would roast a salmon and the women [*sic*; Txemsum's wife] would carefully gather all the bones and the remnants and burn these and as she done this they heard a happy cry in the waters of the stream. This was the salmon they had just ate now restored again." As long as Txemsum respected his wife and her relatives, he had plenty of food.

Unfortunately for Txemsum he grew jealous of his wife and lost his trust in her. His wife

> became very angry. "I'll go away back to my own people as I am afraid you will do me injury." So she went out of the house and called out as she went out "Come my children, come with me." She went down into the stream, into the water and disappeared and all of the dried salmon now became alive and all jumped into the water and became live salmon and swam away after the woman, who was the Princess of the Salmon. Txemsum's supply of salmon was all gone. . . . He was now very hungry with nothing to eat. (Beynon notebook, 1954, "Txemsum and the Salmon" by John Tait (Gispaxlaots), collected by Beynon for M. Barbeau, BF 134.4, CMC)

Jay Miller (1997) describes the results of people not respecting the gifts of their nonhuman relations. In his account of the story of Temlaxham, an ancient Tsimshian community of origin, we learn of how the people are punished for forgetting themselves, for disrespecting their own animal relatives:

> Everyone did as he or she pleased. Great chiefs would give feasts and kill many slaves. They wasted food. The people had become wicked. One day some children went across the Skeena to play by

themselves. One of them went for a drink at a small stream. There he saw many trout. He called to the others, and they began to fish for trout even though they already had plenty of food. They abused the trout. When they caught a fish, they would put urine in its mouth and return it to the water to watch it writhe and die. They laughed and mocked the fish in its agony. The trout had come to spawn that fine spring day, but they died instead. Soon a black fog began and a strong wind blew. Then it began to rain torrents. The trout stream began to rise. The children drowned. (63–64)

Marc Spencer (Ganhada, Gitxaała), in an interview with William Beynon in 1953, described a similar Gitxaała account of a flood brought about by children disrespecting salmon at a village on Banks Island known as K'na'woow (Place of the Snares):

The salmon were very plentiful in all these creeks and the people had plenty. It was then that some of the young people, now having all of the salmon they required, began to abuse the salmon by catching them in looped snares which they made from fine roots. When the salmon's head swam into the loop they would pull it tight and then leave the salmon hanging by the neck half out of water, then the eagles and other preying animals would come and devour the salmon. The older people begged the young people to stop their abuses to the salmon but these would not heed the warnings of the older people and soon other children in the nearby villages began doing the same. Their elders kept warning them 'you will cause the anger of the chief of the Skies, because you are abusing the valuable salmon,' but they would pay no attention to their warnings. Soon the weather began to change and the rain began to come down heavy and soon the rivers began to rise and gradually the waters rose and soon the villages at the creeks became submerged and still the waters rose and soon the small islands became submerged and then the people who up till then had kept moving up into the hills now got everything into their large canoes and the high hills and mountains were now all submerged only here and there were small portions of the hills to which the people were gathering to anchor their canoes and soon these disappeared and the people that were saved began to drift apart. The people knew that this was the revenge of the salmon that caused the flood retaliating after the many abuses. (Beynon notebook, n.d., interview with Mark Spencer, BF 132.5, CMC)

If the salmon or the trout are treated inappropriately, they will leave or exact retribution. If respected, they will reward the harvester. History has taught us that catching too much salmon from a particular location will result in a marked decline or total extirpation of the stock. The same history has also shown that not taking enough seems to have a similar effect. Thus the oral histories provide guidelines for behavior that are reinforced by direct observations of the behavior of fish.

Gitxaała Fisheries in Historical Context

The social relations between people and our nonhuman brethren guided our millennia-long fisheries practices. There is no known time—except during infrequent famines—during which Gitxaała have not harvested marine resources. Archaeological research that we have undertaken documents at least five millennia of harvesting.[1]

From that research we have identified faunal remains at Gitxaała villages and resource harvesting locations of more than one dozen unique species of invertebrates and more than two dozen species of fish, plus a multitude of marine mammals and terrestrial vertebrates and birds (Wigen 2012). Using charcoal samples from the deepest parts of the anthropogenic soils we have dated these faunal remains to over five thousand years old.[2] Over Gitxaała's long history, with rare exceptions, harvest levels have remained remarkably consistent and productive.

Ancient Gitxaała harvesting techniques have included passive and active gear types. Passive (or static) gears are set in place and use the action of fish the or current to trap the target species. Active gears are not fixed in place, and the fisher uses them to actively chase and trap the fish. Passive gears, such as stone and wooden weirs, use tidal action to harvest salmon, herring, and flatfish. Gill nets, originally made from natural plant fibers but today made from nylon, were (and are) set along shorelines or across creek mouths so that migrating fish become trapped within them. Active gears, such as dip nets, gaffs, spears, and drag seines, were used to target fish and animals less likely to be caught by passive techniques. All of these technologies rely upon a fine local understanding of fish behavior and environmental setting in order to work.

Salmon and herring are two of the most important fish harvested in Gitxaała territory. For millennia Gitxaała people have fished herring for their flesh and their roe. Our archaeological investigations in Gitxaała territory since 2009 have revealed the presence of herring bones in the majority of sites for which we have collected faunal samples (Smethurst 2014). As discussed in more detail in chapter 6, herring roe has been harvested by using seaweed, kelp, and hemlock branches. Elders and community members also describe the deliberate planting of herring in certain areas by purposefully towing trees covered in spawn from one area to another in order to seed it for future fishing.

Salmon have been, and continue to be, harvested in traditional house territories that are owned and managed by ranking hereditary leaders. Salmon harvesting techniques include gaffing and spearing, using stone traps and wooden weirs, and using a range of net and hook and line gear types (see chapter 8 for more detail). Salmon, along with herring, constitute close to two-thirds of identifiable fish bones we have recovered in our archaeological research in laxyuup Gitxaała.

Halibut and other bottom fish have been harvested since long before the arrival of Europeans, as seen in early descriptions by Europeans. (Sabaan was fishing halibut, for example, when James Colnett came upon him.) Archaeological evidence indicates that Halibut and other bottom fish, such as various species of rock cod, gray cod, black cod, and lingcod, were a persistent and significant component of precontact diets.[3] Museum collections, such as at New York's American Museum of Natural History, Chicago's Field Museum, and Vancouver's Museum of Anthropology, contain many fine examples of hooks for catching halibut and other bottom fish dating from prior to, at, or just after European contact with Gitxaała.

Halibut was and is dried in thin pieces starting in the month of May. This thin dried fish, called *woks*, is stored for household consumption and also traded with people who either do not fish or do not have access to halibut fishing grounds.

Abalone, clams, cockles, mussels, snails, chitons, and other mollusks as well as sea urchins are harvested throughout the year. Clams and cockles are typically harvested in the winter months at low tide. Some evidence exists of mariculture in the form of extending the intertidal zone through use of rock terraces and thus creating "clam gardens." (See Eldridge and Parker 2007, 15–16 for a description of what may be a clam garden in Prince Rupert Harbor.) Several of the places that I have visited within laxyuup Gitxaała seem more likely designed to facilitate clam and cockle production than the harvesting of fish. However, the two uses are not necessarily mutually exclusive. Site surveys of favored clam and cockle beds within Gitxaała territory indicate the possibility of direct human activity in shaping the beach zone prior to and immediately after European contact.[4] Of all these species abalone retains a special cultural significance (see chapter 7).

Marine mammals are an important Gitxaała food. For those lineages without access to either the Nass or Kemano runs of oolichan, seal oil was their grease. A favored old food, *hadda oola*, is much talked about by contemporary Gitxaała people. Only a few people still make this delicacy of seal intestines stuffed with seal fat and slow-boiled. Techniques for preserving seal and sea lion meat include drying, smoking, jarring, and freezing. Prior to and at the time of European arrival whales were also harvested for food and oil.

The British skipper Charles Bishop sailed from Bristol in 1794 in search of his fortune in the sea otter trade. A year later he came upon Gitxaała. His description of a seal-processing site is the earliest surviving European description of this long-standing Gitxaała harvesting practice (see chapter 3).

Before turning to the changes wrought in Gitxaała's fishery by the arrival of Europeans, one further marine resources merits our attention: seaweed. Seaweed is a longtime and critical staple food of Gitxaała. One of my first memories of food is the pickled kelp my aunt Nettie (Annette Dell, née Gamble, daughter of Edward Gamble and Ellen Gamble, née Denis) gave us. There were other foods, like the annual delivery of oolichan, but the pickled kelp stood out. It is perhaps an unusual example, but it is one that arises from a practice of diverse seaweed harvesting hybridized with European pickling traditions.

Nearly every public meal and feast that I have attended in Lach Klan has had at least one type of food that involves or is based on seaweed. The staple contemporary seaweed is of the *Porphyra* genus. This seaweed is harvested in May on the outer exposed rocks on the seaward portions of Gitxaała's territory. From just outside the village of Lach Klan along the north and west coasts of Porcher Island across to the west coast of Banks Island and then south toward the Estevan Group one can find harvesting places belonging to various Gitxaała walps.

Seaweed is typically dried on the rocks where it is picked or transported back to Lach Klan—or, in earlier years, to one of the other main village sites—for drying on special seaweed boards made from cedar planks. Nancy Turner and Helen Clifton (2006) describe the process as conducted by Gitga'ata, close neighbors to Gitxaała.

In my research with Caroline Butler over the past decade we have interviewed several dozen community matriarchs who have explained in detail seaweed harvesting, processing, and preparing for consumption. Some of this research was focused on the specific ecological knowledge of community members (Butler 2004). Other aspects of our research examined issues of climate change (Ignas and Campbell 2009). Through all of this Gitxaała people express deep pride and pleasure when talking about, sharing, and eating seaweed.

All of these foods were (and are) harvested for domestic consumption and to trade and exchange with people, at times far removed from Gitxaała's own territory. This is a critical aspect of Gitxaała harvests. Community members become rightly incensed when outsiders refer to their harvests as subsistence or mere food fisheries. For Gitxaała the label "subsistence" sounds like an insult, an inference that one is only barely eking out an existence, barely getting by from small numbers of fish. This is quite far from the truth. Gitxaała is a society that values wealth and is focused on a system of rank and prestige based in large measure on the capacity to harvest surpluses. To be labeled a subsistence harvester is to call one impoverished. It is tantamount to a repudiation of Gitxaała conceptions of authority and jurisdiction over the laxyuup. Trade for economic benefit internally and with nations far removed from the central areas of Gitxaała territory is a long-standing critical component of Gitxaała culture and of the Gitxaała practice of fisheries. Without the capacity to harvest surpluses for trade, Gitxaała hereditary leaders are in a real sense diminished.

Trade and Gitxaała Fisheries

Prior to and at the time of European contact, the practice of exchange for benefit was an integral aspect of Gitxaała culture and society. Trade and exchange of abalone, salmon, seaweed, herring roe, cockles, and other items were critical to the function of Gitxaała practices such as the yaawk (feast). The exchange of food and other items such as shells among Gitxaała either at a yaawk or in more explicit trading contexts is trade for economic benefit. It is in these practices that the critical social values of the accumulation of wealth, prestige, and social rank occur and are maintained.

Three types of evidence for trade exist: ethnographic data (including adaawx and published reports), linguistic data (concerning words and phrases used to identify trade items), and archaeological data (regarding distribution of food products).Gitxaała adaawx describe the development of trading relations with neighboring Ts'msyen and others. In the adaawx "The Purchase of the Nauhulk," for example, James Lewis of Kitkatla describes the trading privileges of Ts'msyen and Gitxaała people, as recorded by Beynon: "The Gilodza were privileged to trade with the Haida of what is now Prince of Wales Island. The Gitlan traded with the Nass tribes; the Gitwilgoats, with the Haida of what is now the Queen Charlotte Islands; the Gidzaxlahl and Gitsis with the Tlingit, with whom their royal houses were related; the Gixpaxloats, with the Upper Skeena; the Gitando with the Kitselas; and the Kitkatla with the Kitimat and the Bella Bella. Thus all had exclusive trading areas."[5]

Beynon himself describes the close relations between Gitxaała and the Haida: "When the Gitxaała went fur seal hunting [fur sealing] they frequently went very close to the Haida coast. And at times the relationship between some of the Gitxaała groups and the Haidas was very friendly and often so, to this day there are some of the Gitxaała names are still being used by the Skidigate Haidas such as niswexs, a chiefly name of the T'sibaasa, Gispawudada group."[6]

These adaawx, as discussed elsewhere in this book, include a history of alliances and conflicts.[7] These accounts also document the various types of goods traded between different First Nations and describe who had rights to trade with whom and under what conditions.

Linguistic data (collected by John Dunn, Margaret Anderson, and Bruce Rigsby, among others)[8] can be used to identify terms for trade and exchange and terms for varieties of food products in the Tsimshianic languages. The first set of terms is important in establishing that trade for economic benefit existed. If terms for trade and exchange exist in a language, then it can be inferred that a people were familiar with and very likely engaged in trade. In sm'algyax at least four words can be identified that imply some sort of exchange: *diik* (buy), *'wa'at* (sell), *gilam* (give), and *sagyook* (trade). There are also numerous words for specific types of presents, some obligatory and some repayable.[9] The sm'algyax dictionary lists more than thirty words for various types of exchanges, ranging from gift giving to trade and sale.[10]

The second set of terms (describing a variety of food items) is equally important for demonstrating the existence, or at least the possibility, of trade for economic benefit. For example, there are a variety of terms that describe types of preserved fish (half-smoked, smoked, split and dried, etc.), the run of a fish (early, late, etc.), and variations in aesthetic qualities such as color, texture, and taste. The existence of these terms and concepts indicates the existence of a finely tuned aesthetic appreciation of differences between fish products. Thus there is not simply one type of salmon available to everyone everywhere; rather there are a range of salmon products, some of which are recognized as more desirable than others. This distinction in taste and quality extends to all manner of fish products, including abalone as food and as ceremonial decoration. This form of product differentiation would be important in the establishment of networks of trade in fish products between different communities and households.

Data from archaeological studies also substantiate the significance of fishing and the likelihood of trade prior to European contact. Aside from the work that I have conducted in recent years, very little serious archaeological research has been conducted within Gitxaała territory. There has been some minor work on site identification for consultative processes connected to logging and other development plans. Some work is currently ongoing in the Prince Rupert Harbor area by consultants and university-based researchers. An earlier project, led by George MacDonald, was instrumental in excavating sites along the Skeena River (Coupland 1985) and Prince Rupert Harbor (Ames 2005). Works by R. G. Matson and Gary Coupland (1995) and Kenneth Ames and Herbert Maschner (1999) provide detailed overviews of the state of archaeological knowledge of the Pacific Northwest. Both books describe trade and exchange (primarily as related to prestige items such as obsidian, but other trade goods such as food products are also discussed). However, with the exception of some work by Phillip Drucker (1943) in 1938 and Bjorn Simonsen (1973) in 1969–70, since 2009 the only extended archaeological work within the core Gitxaała territories has been my own.

To date our archaeological work in laxyuup Gitxaała has demonstrated extensive marine harvests of more than forty different marine species. As noted previously, the two most abundant fish identified in our research are salmon and herring. One major village site has extensive quantities of abalone shell, and at least one third of the sites we have examined have significant quantities of sea urchin and chiton. In terms of the material conditions for trade, we have found regional variations in the faunal assemblages that create the potential for regional exchange systems in which one community specializes in abalone, for example, while another focuses on salmon and anchovies. These three lines of evidence contribute to our conclusion that trade was a core cultural aspect of Gitxaała society.

When the early European merchants ventured into Gitxaała territory starting in the late 1700s they found the Gitxaała more than able negotiators who were not satisfied with mere trinkets. They also found that the Gitxaała had a strong sense of proprietorship. (See chapter 2 on these early encounters between Europeans and Gitxaała.) When the Europeans violated Gitxaała protocols by fishing, logging, or using places without properly compensating their Gitxaała hosts, Gitxaała retaliated either with direct physical attacks or with punitive actions the Europeans considered theft. However, when the Europeans stood face to face with Gitxaała and engaged in dialogue, both parties benefited from the Gitxaała history and practice of trade.

Gitxaała and the Contemporary Fishing Industry

Over the course of the late nineteenth through the twentieth century Gitxaała people shifted their commercial fishing operations from trade and exchange for benefit within a long-standing regional Indigenous economic system to participation within an emerging industrial extractive fishing industry. In the early period of contact and during the fur trade Gitxaała people licensed traders to harvest fish and also caught and sold fish products to the visiting fur traders. However, it was with the emergence of the salmon canning industry in the late nineteenth century that Gitxaała involvement in the industrial extractive fishery began in earnest. From the start the industrial fisheries combined with Gitxaała traditional practices and, especially in terms of the drag seine operations, occurred explicitly on and within traditional Gitxaała fishing locations that were owned by named hereditary leaders. Gitxaała fishers adapted to changes in the regulatory and technical structure of the fisheries, yet at each moment of change more and more Gitxaała people have found themselves pushed out of the industrial fishery and restricted in their ability to make a livelihood from their own resources. Nonetheless Gitxaała people maintain an active resource harvesting practice that supplies food internally to community members and externally through a range of commercial practices (some through the licensed industrial fishery, some under the authority and jurisdiction of Gitxaała protocols).

During the late nineteenth century Port Essington, at the confluence of the Ecstall and Skeena rivers, developed as the primary cannery and steamship hub on the Skeena. Port Essington quickly supplanted the Hudson Bay Company trading post in Fort Simpson (just to the north of present-day Prince Rupert) as the economic center of industrial development on the northern BC coast. The extension of the Grand Trunk Railroad to the coast in 1911 created the opportunity to develop Prince Rupert as the commercial capital of the region. Shortly thereafter Prince Rupert gained economic dominance over Port Essington and the aboriginal villages in the region.

These spatial transformations in settlement were only one aspect of the changes wrought by industrial expansion on the north coast.

Gitxaała and other Indigenous peoples provided the bulk of the labor power for the fishing industry on the north coast until the middle decades of the twentieth century. The early development of the fishery was dependent on their participation as local knowledge holders, brokers of labor power, independent producers, and wage laborers. The reserve system and fisheries regulations contributed to a structure that at first encouraged Indigenous production for these industries, and then increasingly restricted Indigenous people from participating in them.

The northern canning industry was quite literally built on the traditional fisheries of the Gitxaała. Some canneries, such as the cannery at K'moda (Lowe Inlet), were located at Gitxaała shore stations and village sites. At other locations the canneries held the commercial fishing permits from the federal government, but most of these permits were actually fished by Gitxaała fishermen in accordance with traditional protocols. During the late nineteenth century the canneries relied on supplies of fish from both their fleet of gillnetters and from the traditional fish camps of Gitxaała chiefs.

Gitxaała fishers had developed an efficient yet sustainable method of harvesting salmon as they returned to their creeks to spawn. Harvested fish were smoked and dried and later traded throughout large commercial networks that extended far beyond the immediate networks of house group or village.

The stone traps were eventually replaced with drag seine nets. A large net was set from a boat and winched into the beach. The drag seine operations employed extended kin to harvest and process various species of salmon. With the establishment of the canneries, the hereditary chiefs, who organized production, integrated the sale of salmon to the canneries into their established patterns of trade, sale, and community consumption.

Gitxaała drag seine operations operated until 1964, when they were officially shut down by the Department of Fisheries and Oceans for "conservation" reasons. However, long before this point the ownership of the drag seine sites, and their associated fishing rights, had been subtly undermined by industrial interests. The canneries obtained legal land titles to many of the drag seine sites by the early years of the twentieth century, even when customary control and ownership were recognized and practiced within the Gitxaała world. It became Department of Fisheries and Oceans policy not to grant seine licenses to Indians, and this persisted until the 1920s (Newell 1993, 54). The canneries continued, however, to recognize chiefly authority over these operations, if only to ensure a reliable supply of fish and labor power. A good example of this is a letter of agreement between Gitxaała chief Paul Sebassah and C. S. Windsor in 1877, allowing Windsor restricted rights to fish and to establish a cannery within Sebassah's territory for a fixed sum of money. These fishing sites were key to the integration of the traditional economy with the capitalist economy, and chiefly power with industrial interests. This general pattern is explored in more detail in the account of K'moda (chapter 8).

While many chiefs and their families spent part of the fishing season at their drag seine operations, the majority of village members began to move to the canneries for fishing and processing employment. The canneries used "village bosses" to recruit fishermen and processing workers. Sometimes whole villages moved to one particular cannery. Elders today recall that Lach Klan was often empty in the summer, with only one elderly man left behind as caretaker.

While the canneries used immigrant Chinese and Japanese workers, who were organized under a labor contractor, they also required the local, seasonal, and relatively inexpensive labor of First Nations women (and their children). Historical sociologist Alicja Muszynski (1996, 89) explains that the canneries could make use of Indians as cheap wage labor because of the traditional subsistence economy's effective subsidy of their low cannery wages. Children's labor was also essential to the cannery system; older children provided child care for infant siblings, and other children assisted their mothers and grandmothers, increasing their income on the piece rate wage. Gitxaała women remember standing on boxes to pass their mothers cans in order to speed up the process. Gitxaała boys stacked the cans and moved boxes for their female kin.

The canneries were also sites for the reproduction of the traditional economy. The canneries became the summertime centers of Indigenous commerce. Families brought their surplus food to trade and sell. The industry drew from both coastal and interior villages and thus provided the opportunity to trade for the particular food specialties of each community. Gitxaała women traded dried herring eggs, abalone, clams, cockles, and seaweed with Gitsxan women for moose meat and berries and with the Nisga'a for oolichan products.

The canneries provided a nexus for Indigenous trade and created new avenues to maintain and develop ancient Indigenous networks in the context of the emerging industrial economy. However, industrial development on the north coast also disrupted and inhibited Gitxaała's economic system. The reserve system and natural resource regulations worked in combination to expropriate Gitxaała land and resources and to transform Gitxaała people into a dependent labor force for the developing industries. Later policy worked to exclude Gitxaała people from the workforce and to replace them with white workers and resource producers.

The official expropriation of First Nations land began with the creation of the first reserve in Victoria Harbor prior to 1852 (see Harris 2002). The reserve system was essentially a tool for opening up land for European settlement and development. In British Columbia the reserves were considerably smaller than in other parts of Canada. The creation of many small reserves in British Columbia was intended to encourage industry, thrift, and materialism and to provide cheap seasonal labor to the industrial economy (Harris 2002, 65). The reserves averaged five hectares per person, compared to allocations of up to 260 hectares in the western interior (Newell 1993, 56), and tended to be placed on or near customary fishing sites. (This is especially the case for coastal reserves.)

The reserve system appears designed to restrict First Nations' access to the resources of most of their traditional territories. In addition First Nations were inhibited from using the resources located on their small reserve holdings. Prior to 1916 the province's reversionary interest in reserve land (in conflict with the Dominion) stunted early development of Indian resources. Until the McKenna-McBride Commission resolved this dispute, the bands could not sell the timber on reserves because the province continued to claim an interest in it (see Harris 2002, 274).

Even after the resolution of provincial claims to reserve timber, the federal government restricted the sale of timber. There is a 1916 memo from the Department of Indian Affairs and Northern Development that suggests the need to restrict the cutting of timber on reserves in order to protect it; later, Circular No. 030-2 in 1934 proposes to restrict the sale of reserve timber to conserve it for Indian use (Menzies and Butler 2001). However, where reserve timber was needed for non-Native development, it could be readily harvested, with little compensation for the band. McDonald (1990, 46) traces the use of Kitsumkalum timber from IR 1 and IR 3 between 1908 and 1910 for the Canadian Trans-Pacific Railroad. The Kitsumkalum were paid 7 percent of the required stumpage for harvesting over two thousand trees from their reserves.

The multiple small reserves allocated to First Nations in BC also reflected the assumption of continued access to fisheries (Newell 1993, 56). Commissioner Peter O'Reilly reserved fishing stations in 1881 for every band he encountered, protecting traditional fishing stations and summer village sites (Harris 2002, 202). Knight (1996, 306) suggests that over half of the reserves in the province were intended for fisheries. However, the Department of Fisheries and Oceans was opposed to exclusive Native fishing rights and instead restricted access to these anticipated resources. The department discouraged the allocation of coastal fishing stations as reserves and refused to allow exclusive Native fisheries access (Harris 2002, 202). Within Gitxaała territory the majority of reserves allocated by O'Reilly were first and foremost fishing or harvesting operations. As discussed earlier, the only general-purpose village sites that were allocated to Gitxaała as reserves were Dolphin Island (the site of Gitxaała's main village, Lach Klan, IR 1) and Citeyats (IR 9). Klapthlon (IR 5 and 5A) was set up as a possible new main village site closer to the steamship routes running along Grenville Channel. All the remaining reserves are near productive sockeye salmon systems (or, in the case of Kul IR 18 on Bonilla Island, a seal harvesting location). It is important to note that there are many other resource harvesting sites that were used by, and remain in use by, Gitxaała, but those assigned by O'Reilly are predominantly salmon harvesting locations.

The most notorious fisheries regulation to limit Gitxaała access to fish within their own territory was the creation of the food fishery under the provisions of the Canadian Fisheries Act. This regulatory structure creates a false distinction between subsistence and commercial fisheries. It has inhibited Gitxaała exercise of their sovereign right to fish for a livelihood in accordance with customary laws for over one hundred years and has hastened their incorporation within the industrial fishery as the primary labor force. In 1888 the Fisheries Act began to differentiate between Indians' right to fish for the purpose of food (which was exempt from certain regulations) and the right to sale and barter. The underlying assumption of this regulatory structure is that selling fish is not an Indian tradition; this has been used to exclude First Nations harvesters from establishing our own aboriginal commercial fishery.

In addition to the legislation of Indian fishing as a subsistence activity, there were increasing restrictions on the access of First Nations to fish. Restrictions on on the Skeena began within a year of the establishment of the first cannery on the river (McDonald 1994, 164); the regulation worked to remove fish from the traditional economy in favor of the industrial economy. The provincial and federal governments entered into a memorandum of understanding in 1912 to create a fishery dominated by white settlers.[11] Up until that time the large fish companies on the north coast maintained exclusive control over federally issued fishing permits, referred to as the "boat rating system." Under this system each of the established canneries worked out a distribution of fishing effort among themselves. The companies then distributed their permits to reliable fishermen in such a way as to control the supply of fish to their canneries. On the north coast this meant that the majority of fishermen remained First Nations, including many Gitxaała fishers who specialized in drag seining and then, in later years, in mobile seiners and gillnetters.

By the early twentieth century the gold rush period of the fishery had come to an end. Those companies that survived and consolidated during the turbulent early years found themselves in possession of a virtual license to print money. The fact that they in effect controlled harvesting capacity through the boat rating system made it next to impossible for emerging settler businessmen to break into the fishing industry. For the growing white settler electorate in the province of BC the boat rating system, which placed control of fishing permits in the hands of the established fish companies, posed a linked racial and economic problem. It is important to make very clear that the electorate in BC throughout the period here described was primarily white, male, and propertied. Thus the people who could vote were those who had a direct economic stake in shaping the racial complexion of the fishing industry. The established companies, however, were quite satisfied with their reliance on First Nations fishers and women. This system served to tie Indigenous fishers to the companies and solved the dual problems of maintaining a seasonal labor force and a regular supply of fish.

From the perspective of the primarily white male propertied electorate, however, the established canners' system excluded them from the economic opportunities of the fishery. For them the clearest path to partaking in the riches of the fishery involved breaking the large canneries' monopoly over fishing opportunities by creating a class of independent white fishermen. Thus the following clause in the memorandum of understanding: "It is eminently desirable to have the fisheries carried on by a suitable class of white fishermen. . . . The Fishery Regulations and the policy of both Departments should have in view hastening the time as much as possible when such will be the case."[12]

The memorandum of understanding goes on to lament that while desirable, the creation of a white-only fishery "will require some years." In the interval the memorandum of understanding set out the procedures whereby a guaranteed number of independent licenses would be held for "bona fide white fishermen." The agreement further set up the provision that "the reservation [of permits] will be sufficient to cover all applications from bona fide white fishermen." Explicit and otherwise, the regulations, such as the 1912 memorandum of understanding, that governed the establishment of fishing during the late nineteenth and early twentieth centuries worked to exclude Indigenous peoples as full participants and owners in the market economy, relegating them to sources of labor power to be extracted like the natural resources of fish, trees, and minerals.

During the middle of the twentieth century Gitxaała people were gradually being excluded from the fishing industry. Anthropologist Michael Kew (1989) suggests that First Nations participation in the fishing industry as owner-operators peaked around the time of World War II. It is primarily the participation of northern Native fishermen that kept the numbers up; as on the Fraser River, aboriginal fishermen were gradually displaced and replaced after 1900 (see Knight 1996).

The increasing capitalization of the fishing fleet put Gitxaała fishers at a disadvantage. Unable to obtain credit based on property (due to the reserve system), they were less able to keep up with the technological advances, including the shift to motorized boats in the early twentieth century. Indigenous fishermen were thus kept closely tied to the canneries for credit and for boats. Increasingly they were operating cannery-owned vessels. This prevented many from enjoying the advantages offered by independent fishermen's organizations such as the Prince Rupert Fishermen's Co-operative (see Menzies 1993, 1996). Their ability to effectively negotiate fish prices was also restricted. Dependence on the canneries as a source of credit and boats eventually contributed to the decline in Native participation in the fishing industry. As the canneries steadily consolidated and centralized after the 1930s, they offered less and less employment to First Nations. In the north, cannery closures between 1944 and 1953 fired 50 percent of the women processing fish (Muszynski 1996, 204).

In 1968 the Davis Plan, named after the minister of fisheries at the time, restructured the commercial fishing industry in BC. License limitation was introduced, which increased the value of salmon licenses and resulted in heavy capitalization of the fleet. The policy shift also prompted the rapid centralization of salmon processing. Women lost their jobs, men lost their boats, and families lost their source of credit.

First Nations fishermen were forced out of the industry at higher rates than non-Indigenous fishermen. Government programs to support First Nations fishermen during the 1970s failed to counteract the losses. Their participation dropped to 29 percent by the early 1990s (Gislason et al. 1996). Communities like Gitxaała, which had enjoyed 100 percent employment (although seasonal) until the 1960s, found themselves without jobs for the first time.

The fishing industry underwent further restructuring in the late 1990s. License buybacks were initiated to reduce the fleet capacity. First Nations fishermen who had persisted in the industry were vulnerable, and many were forced to sell their licenses due to their debt load.

Communities like Gitxaała lost up to 14 percent of their employment during this latest policy shift.

Today a handful of community members hold Canadian commercial fishing licenses and own or operate their own vessels. The band also owns some licenses and its own fishing vessel. A number of community members continue to work as crew members on fishing boats, and both men and women work on a seasonal basis in the few fish plants that remain in Prince Rupert. However, fishing continues to be critical to Gitxaała identity. Many community members retain access to small skiffs and outboards and now use these as their primary basis of operations for fishing within their traditional territories. Proceeds of these fishing and harvesting operations are distributed within the community and are exchanged for benefits within and beyond the community in accord with the authority and jurisdiction of Gitxaała laws and history.

6

Tsk<u>a</u>h, Xs'waanx

Herring, Herring Roe

My first memory of herring is seeing a photo of my infant self when I was about eight years old. My father was holding me in his arms as he stood in the middle of a deckload of herring. The seventy-foot seine boat was plugged to the gunnels with fish. My father fished on a herring seine boat during the 1960s. These large boats used seine nets to catch herring from which was produced animal feed and fertilizer (hard to imagine the waste of such a good fish). While it was a good living for a young fisherman with a family, it was devastating to the coastal herring stocks, which collapsed by the end of the 1960s.

A good friend of my father's and a fellow fisherman, the late George Wood, described the devastating effects of the reduction herring fishery this way: "I joined the reduction herring fishery near the end of its time, and fished for the last five years that fishing was open. The reduction herring fishery was eventually shut down on the coast because it nearly wiped out the herring stocks in British Columbia. Part of the reason for the herring collapse at that time was that we used lights to fish for the herring. We would harvest whatever the boat could hold. I personally saw hundreds and hundreds of tons of herring pulled from the waters during the reduction fishery."

Like my father, George fished on boats that were affiliated with the Prince Rupert Fishermen's Co-op. I had first met George when he was a crew member on the *Brooks Bay* (skippered by Tommy Mosley) in the late 1970s, when I was a young man working on my father's boat. Later, when I was doing research in Lach Klan, I had many opportunities to speak with him informally and, on occasion, to conduct formal interviews with him about his life in BC's commercial fishery.

My father has described to me the amazing variation of herring from inlet to inlet, cove to cove. In some locations all the fish were large; in other places they were a mixture of sizes or small. The sheen of the fish was also different from place to place: some were oilier, others drier. The common theme of his stories, however, was that the fishermen loaded their boats as much as they could and took their catch to port, where it was reduced to animal feed.

Indigenous peoples harvested herring for thousands of years prior to the industrial herring fishery. In our archaeological research in laxyuup Gitxaała we have found herring to be as important a constituent of the faunal assemblage as is salmon. For archaeologists and contemporary Gitxaała harvesters alike, this was a surprising result. Yet prior to the reduction herring fishery era, herring were ubiquitous, according to the historical documents and oral accounts, so we should not be surprised (McKechnie et al. 2014). This chapter explores the importance of herring for Gitxaała yesterday and today and examines the intriguing narrowing of the utilization of this fish that has occurred since the arrival of K̲'amksiwa̲h.

Historical Utilization

Historical accounts clearly document the harvesting of herring throughout British Columbian waters. Early travelers' accounts include references to herring, among other fish, being dried and smoked. Franz Boas's (1921) famous accounts of the Kwakwaka'wakw describe in fine detail the range of harvesting and processing techniques.

Herring was harvested by using both passive and active gear. Intertidal stone traps were built along shorelines herring frequented during spawning season. Using the behavior of the fish (herring is a schooling fish, and hundreds, if not thousands, of tons will congregate in one school) and the action of tide, these stone traps would create the conditions to trap fish for harvest. Active gears for herring included a rake-like device that was armed with sharp teeth. Fishers using this method would maneuver their canoes over a school of herring, pull the rake through the school, impaling the herring, and then shake them off into the canoe. The herring was then processed by drying, smoking, or rendering into oil.

The fresh herring was strung through their gills on prepared cedar skewers, a couple of feet in length, in groups of fifty to one hundred fish. These fish-laden skewers were then hung in the rafters of a longhouse to dry or processed in a specially built smokehouse. Once either dried or smoked the fish was packaged in bentwood boxes for long-term storage. Herring processed in this manner was used as a household food item and as a commodity for trade and exchange.

The method for rendering herring into oil is similar to that used to produce oolichan grease. After capture the herring were stored in large wooden containers and allowed to ripen for a period of several days or weeks. Once ripe the fish were boiled in large open containers, and the oil floated to the surface of the water. The resultant fish oil was then stored in special wooden boxes and consumed as a household food item or traded in the regional networks of trade and exchange.

Herring roe was, and remains, a food item harvested for household consumption and trade. To harvest roe a work group would first collect hemlock branches or entire small trees. The branches would be secured along the shoreline in anticipation of the spawning herring, usually from April through May. A second form of herring roe, called *legi*, was also harvested. This is a variant of spawn on seaweed; it is picked at low tide after the herring have spawned. While most Gitxaała herring roe harvested today comes from Kitkatla Inlet near Lach Klan, in years past roe (and herring) were harvested throughout laxyuup Gitxaała.

Herring roe is processed to store by drying. In the case of roe on hemlock, the branches are removed from the water once the spawning fish have deposited a layer of spawn. On shore the branches are cut into smaller lengths, which are hung to air-dry the roe. Once dried, the roe is carefully removed from the branches and, in the past, was packed in bentwood boxes for storage. Today people use plastic bags and freeze the dried roe to store for future use. Legi is dried and stored in the same manner.

For millennia prior to the arrival of K'amksiwah herring was harvested for roe and the fish itself. Based on our archaeological research we can document very clearly the importance of herring in the recovered faunal assemblages. Our research began in 2008 with the objective of mapping and recording intertidal fish traps. Beginning in 2009 we expanded our scope to include a set of noninvasive archaeological techniques: systematic soil sampling by bucket auger, percussion coring, and limited small excavations (about one cubic meter) of cooking hearths in the ancient longhouses. Our objective was to document the deep history of Gitxaała harvest practices as a complement to contemporary historical knowledge provided by community resource harvesters and elders.

The percussion coring allows us to determine the depth of anthropogenic soils at the places of our research and whether the place had been lived in without interruption. We also are able to collect charcoal samples from the very bottom of the core tests and use them to determine the date of earliest occupation through the process of c14 dating. The household hearth excavations provide us with a fine-grained analysis of food processing. The augers have been our primary technique for developing a systematic understanding of Gitxaała's ancient harvesting practices.

With the auger we are able to collect soil samples from the surface to the bottom of the anthropogenic soils. The auger is screwed into the ground in thirty-centimeter intervals. Each insertion of the auger produces about one liter of soil, which is collected in plastic bags for later screening and analysis at the Museum of Anthropology at the University of British Columbia. Depending on the depth of the soil we can find ourselves collecting samples from as deep as five or even six meters! We place our test holes about ten to fifteen meters apart from each other (depending on the size of the place we are documenting) in a systematic grid pattern. Using this approach we can provide a fairly detailed account of the faunal materials deposited at each place we visit. We are able to locate each sample in a spatial and temporal matrix. Doing all of this has provided us with a very detailed account of the wide diversity of animals harvested over time. Most significant to me is the consistency of harvest at each location over multiple millennia.

In archaeology one of the standard measures used is NISP: number of individual specimens. NISP is often presented as a percentage to allow for comparisons of relative abundance of a particular species within the context of a specific sample or archaeological site. It is important to point out that NISP is not a measure of abundance of species or a measure of the actual harvest level. It simply tells us that a species was present and its relative quantity in relation to other species indentified in a sample.

Table 1 shows the %NISP of salmon, herring, and greenling for nine Gitxaała places we have worked at since 2009. The amazing thing here is the quantity of herring relative to the culturally iconic fish, salmon. These data allow us to talk about seasonality of use (herring is typically a spring fish and salmon a summer and fall fish) and regional networks of exchange. For our purposes here, the data point to the use of whole herring by Gitxaała in the past.

K'moda has a lower, almost insignificant %NISP for herring compared to the other sites. However K'moda has a high %NISP for a herring-like fish, anchovy. The two places at Will u sgetk have relatively low %NISP herring but a correspondingly high rockfish %NISP. Regional variations in faunal assemblages speak to the potential of interregional trade. Ultimately our data show that herring was an important fish consumed whole in the millennia prior to the arrival of K̲'amksiwa̲h. I now turn to an examination of the factors and processes that resulted in a narrowing of herring utilization by Gitxaała.

Narrowing of Utilization

Herring is not alone among traditional Gitxaała food items that have seen changed patterns of utilization. Some foods are no longer used; new items have been added (some of which, such as sugar, flour, and rice, have quite deleterious health effects); and long-standing food items are today more likely to be fried rather than boiled or baked, as they were in the past. Changing foodways are part of all cultures. Understanding how and why a specific change in taste or practice has occurred at a specific location or a particular moment in time is critically important. Some changes in taste are merely shifts in fashion; others can tell us about structural alterations or disruptions. Changes in utilization of herring point to a structural change in Gitxaała society induced by incorporation within the global capitalist economy.

Some food items require a high investment of human labor. Some

Table 1. *Percent NISP of salmon, herring, and greenling for nine Gitxaała villages*

PLACE	SALMON (%NISP)	HERRING (%NISP)	GREENLING (%NISP)
Citeyats	71.36	9.47	5.30
K'moda[1]	76.59	0.8	0.48
Ks'waan	33.24	27.06	27.74
Ktsm laagn	33.52	56.82	0.57
Lax kn dip wand	21.64	68.06	6.11
Lax kwil da'a	54.45	37.72	1.78
Sga wina'a	23.61	62.14	7.8
Will u sgetk (1)	51.43	14.34	9.56
Will u sgetk (2)[2]	15.15	16.67	16.67

1 K'moda is the only place to show a high %NISP for anchovy, 21.34. Anchovy shows up in trace amounts at two other places, both of which are some distance away, on the west coast of Banks Island.

2 For Will u sgetk (2) the %NISP of rockfish is 39.39. This is one of the highest values for rockfish. The next highest is nearby Will u sgetk (1), with a %NISP of 21.22.

produce a comparatively low energy output compared to other foods. Some require complicated procedures to render the food consumable. Herring is a reasonably easy fish to catch given the harvesting gear utilized by Gitxaała and the behavior of the fish. It is, however, a fish that required a relatively high intensity of labor power to harvest usable quantities. Relative to salmon and halibut—two other important fish—herring requires more effort per unit harvested. Said differently, less effort catches more salmon and more halibut using traditional fishing gears. This point is critical, I think, when one considers the human implications of initial contact with the Ḵ'amksiwaḥ.

As Robert Boyd (1999) documents in chilling detail, Ḵ'amksiwaḥ contact brought with it a pathogenic tidal wave of death. From the mid-1700s to the early 1900s waves of smallpox, measles, and influenza swept along the coast. These waves of death disrupted social relations and human communities. Gitxaała oral history has several accounts of having to resort to mass graves to cope with the large numbers of deaths in some of the outlying villages.

Early ships' logs, in particular that of Charles Bishop on the sailing vessel *Ruby*, document the spread and impact of diseases circa 1795. The following is Bishop's entry for Saturday, July 27, 1795:

> In the Afternoon, Shakes [Seax] in a large Cannoe Paddled by 20 men with his two wives, his son, and Several Other chiefs, Attended by 2 Large cannoes full of Amr'd Men, and the Cannoe which had been with us in the Morning, came Paddling down to the Ship, Singing, with Great Melody. . . . Shakes appear'd to be about 40 years of age and was a respectable Figure, but the Small Pox with which he was covered, though it appeared to be in the latest stages of the disorder, rendered him a Piteous object. (Roe 1967, 70–71)

A month later Captain Bishop again visited Seax. Bishop comments:

> The Small Pox is raging among them and altho' shakes is quite recovered, yet his Family are much affected by it and he has buried one of his Wives lately. His Eldest and favourite son is now ill of this terrible desease. (91–92)

Disease was spread not simply by the accident of contact. In 1862 local officials in Victoria forcibly evicted Indigenous people from the town when smallpox broke out (Campbell 2005, 94–96). The spread of smallpox from this one event had a devastating effect in coastal communities that had already been weakened by nearly a century of K̲'amksiwa̲h diseases. Gitxaała's population had been devastated by earlier waves of disease and now consisted of barely a thousand people. The 1862 epidemic killed 67 percent of the people living at that time (96).

The impact of depopulation—large and catastrophic waves of death—cannot be ignored when one examines the shift in utilization of herring and other foodstuffs. Disease directly reduced the number of people available for and capable of engaging in the processing of foods and the maintenance of Gitxaała society. This was a common coastal experience in the northwest coast of North America.

With the devastation of disease also came new economic opportunities. I am uncertain as to whether this is an irony or a paradox; it is at the very least a tragedy. The very sailors who brought smallpox into Gitxaała homes were also seeking out furs and commercial trade. Gitxaała was not alone in meeting these new opportunities by redeploying the labor power remaining into economically viable pursuits. In the late 1700s and early 1800s this involved deploying labor into intensified community harvests of sea otters. With the extirpation of sea otters labor was again redeployed to intensify the harvest of seals. Then again, toward the late 1880s, with the rise of the industrial salmon cannery fisheries, labor was redeployed to expand harvesting in salmon fisheries. Throughout all of this the harvesting of herring shifted from a broad-based utilization of oil, flesh, and roe to a narrowly focused fishery targeting only the harvesting of roe.

The transition arose from a combination of reduced availability of labor, changing market opportunities, and the value of roe and flesh of herring compared to other possible foodstuffs. As described previously, harvesting herring for the flesh is labor-intense, whereas herring roe is a relatively easily harvested food item. In the face of the labor shortage strategic decisions were required. These conditions, combined with the new market opportunities, underlie the shift from broad-based to narrow utilization.

The transition was not immediate. However, it would appear that by the late 1800s herring was being harvested by Gitxaała only as roe on an annual basis from April to May. Oral histories of resource harvest in the twentieth century present the harvesting of herring roe, xs'waanx, as one of a normal and important set of activities practiced at spring seaweed camps. Herring roe is further referenced as a critical object of trade within Gitxaała but, more important, with upriver Indigenous communities.

Ben Hill, who spent his childhood springs at a drag seine and seaweed camp on the west coast of Banks Island in the mid-1900s, described how his family would dry roe at their camps. Matthew Hill, who spent his childhood in the same region, describes harvesting herring roe prior to the start of salmon fishing, along with the production of seaweed and fishing for halibut. Larry Bolton, whose house territory is also on the west coast of Banks Island, explains that harvesting herring roe in his laxyuup is important as it is used to trade with people on the Nass for oolichan grease. The herring spawn, he notes, is also a time to hunt birds and ducks that are attracted to the spawn. Few of the harvesters I have spoken with over the past decades—except those, like my father, who fished for herring commercially—ever discussed fishing herring for food. Those who spoke of herring were speaking of herring roe, xs'waanx, not the fish itself.

Contemporary Utilization

Harvesting xs'waanx and the commercial roe-on-kelp fishery are the extent of Gitxaała's contemporary herring fishery. Much of this harvest now takes place in Kitkatla Inlet and along the west coast of Banks Island. Modest harvests occur from time to time in other locations within laxyuup Gitxaała, but the primary harvest area is the Inlet.

Fishermen like my father and George Wood spent their lives working in the commercial fisheries while also maintaining connections to their home communities. George, for example, spent much of the later years of his life fishing on boats operated or owned by the Gitxaała Nation. George fished for commercial roe herring in Kitkatla Inlet from about the 1980s for a decade and then shifted to the roe-on-kelp fishery on Gitxaała's own boat.

A commercial roe-on-kelp and sac roe fishery was established in BC a few years after the collapse of the reduction herring fishery. The roe fishery ushered in a gold rush–like ten-year period in BC's commercial fisheries. The commercial roe fishery exported roe to Japan for prices that rose astronomically during the 1970s and then collapsed just as quickly in the early 1980s.

George witnessed the transformations of the local commercial fishery firsthand:

The first year I started fishing for roe herring in Kitkatla Inlet, two boats would take 1200 tonnes of herring between them. The next year, there were four to six boats which took 800–900 tonnes. Each year after that, the number of boats and tonnage increased until the roe herring fishery was closed. When we fished in Kitkatla Inlet using a seine and pumps, we greatly disturbed the bottom of the Inlet. The nets would drag along the bottom tearing out the eel grass and other marine life in the Inlet. At first, it did not seem to make a big difference to the state of the Inlet. Today, I can now see what kind of impact the commercial roe herring fishery has had on the Inlet. For example, for approximately the last ten years I have not seen any herring spawn in the areas that used to be plentiful in the Inlet and Freeman Pass.[1]

Though some Gitxaała fishers with a foothold in the commercial fishery benefited from the herring gold rush, most community members did not. The effect on Gitxaała's local fishery has been harsh. The industrial reduction fishery, while engaged in overfishing, did not focus on herring stocks in Kitkatla Inlet. The commercial roe fishery, however, did concentrate activities in these waters. The intensity of the commercial fishery in the Inlet made the harvesting of xs'waanx increasingly difficult. Community members report serous declines in availability and quality of xs'waanx since the development of the commercialized roe fishery.

In the spring of 1980 I was a crew member on a commercial herring seine boat. I had previously fished with my father and his crew gillnetting for herring nearly every Spring Break since the mid-1970s; I always appreciated the extended break from school. This was my first season herring seining. (I worked about a half-dozen herring seine seasons over the course of the 1980s.) My job was to operate the twenty-foot power skiff that helped tow, open, and close the seine in partner with the main vessel.

The weather was miserable: strong southeast wind and sheeting, cold rain. It was April. I waited in the skiff, which was tied to the stern of the main boat, as we cruised around the Inlet searching for a large school of herring. The anticipation is akin to standing on a starting line waiting for the starter pistol's shot. But here there is no ready, set . . . It's wait, wait, GO!

When the signal came, the main boat belched a cloud of black smoke, heeling over to one side as she accelerated around and toward the school of fish. I slammed my skiff into reverse, pulling the net off the stern of the main boat. Start to finish was less than ten minutes. And then I sat at the end of a towline holding the main boat in position as the seine was gathered up and the fish loaded on board.

I could see starfish, rocks, and mud coming up with the net. I knew from the radiophone with me in the skiff that we had a good set, maybe a hundred tons. That season the seine fleet took about 2,400 tons and the gill net fleet a further 1,200 tons. We loaded our fish, lifted our skiff, and headed home to Prince Rupert.

The commercial seine fishery and subsequent roe-on-kelp fishery took a heavy toll on the Kitkatla Inlet herring stocks that ultimately was felt by Gitxaała community harvesters. It came to a head in the early 1990s, when Chief Councilor Matthew Hill sued the federal government on behalf of Gitxaała seeking an end to the commercial harvest of herring from the Inlet in order to protect community harvests of xs'waanx. The court didn't provide a remedy that met with Gitxaała's needs and allowed the fishery to continue.

In the legal proceedings Gitxaała argued that community members had not been able to harvest sufficient herring roe for their needs in the years prior to their court action in 2000. The nature of the fishery was such that the commercial roe herring fishery preceded the aboriginal fishery for xs'waanx. The result was that the constitutionally protected aboriginal right to harvest xs'waanx was constantly disrupted by commercial overfishing that took place prior to the aboriginal spawn fishery. To make matters worse the shallow waters of the Inlet combined with the commercial fishing gear resulted in the environmental degradation of the herring spawning habitat. All of this resulted in declining Gitxaała xs'waanx harvests.

The judge, however, was not convinced that he should act: "I am not persuaded that the harm feared by the applicants [Gitxaała] is established as likely to occur. Moreover, should it occur I am not persuaded that it would be irreparable in the circumstances of this case." Paradoxically the judge was blinded to the documented century-long decline of herring stocks in Kitkatla Inlet. Focusing on a narrow interpretation of the law, he decided "the balance of convenience favours the respondent [the minister of fisheries], and those acting on his behalf, and the Court had no basis to interfere with his and their exercise of public statutory responsibilities."[2]

In subsequent years the Department of Fisheries and Oceans has taken a more conservative approach toward the commercial herring fisheries in the Inlet. Nonetheless the commercial herring fishery is still managed in a manner that is injurious to Gitxaała community fisheries. Problems such as this will unfortunately persist until Gitxaała are able to exercise our own authority and jurisdiction unmolested by external interests.

Summary

Any public meal or feast in Lach Klan is guaranteed to have herring roe on the table. Though the flesh of the herring is no longer consumed, herring roe remains a prized staple. The practice of harvesting, preparing, and consuming xs'waanx is integral to being Gitxaała today. Herring roe is a prized trade good that brings cherished foods, such as oolichan grease, into the community. Like abalone and salmon, herring is a central fish in the life and culture of Gitxaała. It has been so for millennia and, as long as external commercial operations, oil tankers, and other industrial developments are kept at bay, it will remain so for millennia to come.

7

Bilhaa

Abalone

Bilhaa is one of a set of Gitxaała culturally important species that "play a unique role in shaping and characterizing the identity of the people who rely on them. . . . These are species that become embedded in a people's cultural traditions and narratives, their ceremonies, dances, songs, and discourse" (Garibaldi and Turner 2004, 1). Until the late twentieth century Gitxaała people were unhindered in the harvesting of bilhaa within their traditional territory and in accord with long-standing systems of Indigenous authority and jurisdiction. However, the rapid expansion of a commercial dive fishery in the 1970s and 1980s brought bilhaa stocks perilously close to extinction. The Department of Fisheries and Oceans (DFO) responded to this self-induced crisis by closing the total bilhaa fishery; it made no effort to accommodate Indigenous interests.

The closure of bilhaa fishing has left a palpable sense a grief among Gitxaała people, especially community elders who have grown up with bilhaa as a key item of food and trade. Community members feel embittered that once again a significant part of their normal lives has been closed to them by the Canadian government. Since the arrival of the first European in our midst Gitxaała people have made clear the extent and nature of our rights, use, and occupancy of our territories. From the yaawk (feasts) held for the ships' skippers James Colnett and Jacinto Caamano in the eighteenth century through the various visitations of government officials, Gitxaała and our leadership have plainly expressed our long ownership of these territories and the rights to use and profit from them. The exclusion from harvesting bilhaa is for Gitxaała just one more attempt to marginalize and exclude us from our ability to carry out our normal livelihood practices.

When I first began professional research with Gitxaała in 1998 I heard over and over a story that I came to call "the abalone story." The pervasive and ubiquitous nature of this story led me to write about it in an article published in the *Canadian Journal of Native Education* in 2004:

> At the heart of the account was a government sponsored research project into the health and location of abalone conducted in the recent past. The government researchers explained that their project would benefit the local community. This would be accomplished by collecting location and population data that would make the job of protecting the abalone grounds from over harvesting and poaching more effective. After some consideration community members agreed and a number of surveys were completed. Following the departure of the researchers a fleet of commercial dive boats turned up on the abalone grounds that had been described to the researchers. The end result was the complete degradation of the local grounds and ultimately a complete closure of commercial abalone fishing on the coast. The community members who had participated in the study felt betrayed by the process. (Menzies 2004, 22)

I go on to discuss the story as a cautionary tale for researchers, as that was the audience for whom I was writing the article. The story is also an account of the community's real and heartfelt loss and sense of betrayal. For generation upon generation community members have harvested seafood in a way that our ancestors have before us. Attempts have been made to accommodate non-Gitxaała in business, in research, and in settlement, but it would seem that each instance has left the community worse off than it was before.

The abalone story reminds us that the impact on Gitxaała people is more than just a loss of a favored food—it is part of an ongoing colonial entanglement of disruption, resistance, and accommodation. Nonetheless, over the past two centuries the practice of fishing, including

for bilhaa, has remained highly significant to Gitxaała. Fishing constitutes a critical component, alongside the harvesting and processing of
terrestrial resources, of what it is to be Gitxaała. The products of harvesting from the sea and intertidal zones are used for food, clothing,
medicine, ceremonial items, and, importantly, trade. The ability to engage in trade and exchange has always been an integral aspect of
Gitxaała culture and society.

Gitxaała people have continued to engage in fisheries since European arrival. While maintaining the continuity of this practice we have
also actively adapted new technologies and techniques of harvesting,
processing, and trading of a variety of seafood, including fin fish, sea
mammals, invertebrates and mollusks of various types (such as bilhaa,
clams, cockles, mussels, barnacles, crabs, chitons, sea cucumbers, sea
urchins), and seaweed and kelp. Government policies, regulations, and
related systematic attempts to displace Gitxaała and other Indigenous
peoples from their traditional territories have contributed additional
pressure for change.

Canadian fisheries policy has developed historically to displace and
marginalize Indigenous fisheries (see Newell 1993). As with all human
societies, however, change in the organization of production does not
in and of itself mean that a society or culture ceases to exist. Nor does
it mean that fisheries cease to be a relevant culturally integral aspect
of being Gitxaała. In fact the various attempts over the past century
and a half to remove Gitxaała from fisheries have not been uniform in
application. For the most part those resources that escaped the gaze
of outsiders remained generally under the control of Gitxaała. Until
the mid-1970s bilhaa was one of those resources that remained outside
of the regulatory gaze of the Canadian state.

Bilhaa Harvesting, Processing, and Use

The Gitxaała practice of bilhaa harvesting has been explicitly organized
to ensure the continuation of the biological stock. Gitxaała harvesting
practices reflect the culturally important role of bilhaa as a treasured
entity, a social being with whom we share relations, and as an important cultural marker of being a ranked member of Gitxaała society. The
effect of this relationship is to place a cultural limitation on the har-

vesting of bilhaa. Bilhaa have been harvested as far back as any living person can recall and prior to the time of European contact (Butler 2004). Evidence for the antiquity of bilhaa harvesting can be found in references to bilhaa in Ts'msyen and Gitxaała adaawx, contemporary academic publications (such as faunal analysis from north coast archaeological sites),[1] and contemporary accounts.

Adaawx, Ceremonial Practice, and Use of Bilhaa

References to the presence, power, and importance of bilhaa to Ts'msyen and Gitxaała people are recorded in the adaawx and are used on ceremonial regalia to denote power and prestige. The cultural importance of bilhaa plays a role in shaping resource-harvesting practices. In combination with the principle of *syt güülum goot* (being of one heart) the high value placed on bilhaa as a symbol of prestige and rank imposes a cultural limitation on harvesting levels. This is so in two ways. First, the use of bilhaa as decoration and adornment is restricted to a minority of high-ranking community members. Second, the cultural importance of bilhaa as a signifier of rank obligates harvesters to treat bilhaa with respect such that unrestrained harvesting is a violation of social norms and is subject to community sanction.

Throughout Gitxaała and Ts'msyen adaawx are accounts of how bilhaa and bilhaa-adorned objects become important cultural markets. For example, "Explanation of the Abalone Bow" is an adaawx that describes how the Bilhaa Bow became a chief's crest (Boas 1916, 284, 835). In the narrative G-it-na-gun-a'ks bilhaa also feature as an inlay on "a good-sized box" that is one of several gifts exchanged between a naxnox, Na-gun-a'ks, and the people of Dzagam-sa'gisk (285–92). Drawing upon his work up to 1916, Boas also notes that "ear-ornaments of abalone shell" are mentioned in the Ts'msyen adaawx (398). Viola Garfield (1939, 194) writes that "at any ceremonial large wool ornaments with abalone shell pendants were worn in the ears of the women who sing in the chief's choir, so that the status of each was clearly indicated to the tribes at large."

Bilhaa is clearly a marker of high rank and prestige within Ts'msyen and Gitxaała society. Halpin (1984) documents how crests that were restricted to high-ranked individuals often had names that would include "shining," and the individuals' associated regalia might use bilhaa shells to indicate their high status. In a description of a mid-nineteenth-century feast Halpin writes, "We would have noted that the men who made the speeches wore the more elaborate headdresses, richly decorated with shining abalone" (16; see also Halpin 1973).

Jay Miller (1997) further highlights the cultural importance of brilliance and luminosity, of light, beams of light, and spirit, or naxnox powers or beings. According to Miller, "The use of abalone, copper, and polished surfaces on chiefly artifacts provides further support for the mediation of light" (39). John Cove's (1987) monograph on Ts'msyen shamanism and narrative also discusses the cultural concept of brilliance, this time in reference to special rock and water mirrors. Bilhaa shells were incorporated into this cultural complex as a critical material manifestation of cultural history and spiritual practices of Ts'msyen and Gitxaała peoples.

Contemporary Academic Accounts

The archaeological and related peer-reviewed publications on the subject of bilhaa are sparse but illuminating in their discussion of the importance of bilhaa to the Ts'msyen peoples, of which academic accounts typically include the Gitxaała. Halpin and Seguin (1990, 271) list bilhaa as one of the shellfish gathered by the Ts'msyen. Quoting Halpin (1984), they write, "Special crests that could be made of real animal heads and skins, and [that] included ermine and abalone decoration, were restricted to the chief" (1990, 276).

In a survey of shellfish harvesting,[2] gender, and status, Madonna Moss (1993, 633) lists bilhaa as one of several shellfish harvested with a prying stick from the low-tide zone (see also Suttles 1990, 28). Richard Bolton (2007), working with Andrew Martindale on Dundas Island, identifies, among other shellfish, bilhaa shell as a constituent of shell middens that date to times prior to European arrival.

Archaeologist Michael Blake (2004, 109–11) has found empirical evidence of bilhaa ornaments dating back more than 1,400 years in a burial mound in the lower Fraser River region. Blake's work complements the ethnographic descriptions of Boas and others on the cultural importance and antiquity of bilhaa use among the Indigenous peoples of the Northwest Coast region.

Prior to my own work in laxyuup Gitxaała, practically no archaeological research had been conducted in this region. The closest sustained archaeological research in this region has centered on Prince Rupert Harbor, where, in the 1960s, George MacDonald began an ambitious program of excavation. In the absence of detailed work elsewhere on the north coast of BC, the Prince Rupert Harbor research has developed into an orthodox vision in which the harbor is seen as the central area of habitation and economic activity outside of the mouth of the Skeena River.

In our archaeological research within Gitxaała territory a fragment of abalone shell was found in a shovel test at an ancient Gitxaała village site in Curtis Inlet. According to Gitxaała adaawx, this is where the important hereditary leader Ts'ibasaa first established his village within Gitxaała territory. We have also found significant quantities of abalone shell in situ at Ks'waan (near Calamity Bay, at the south end of Banks Island). Abalone has been recovered from a one-cubic-meter excavation of a house floor, from a soil profile taken from the exposed shoreward midden face, and from systematic auger tests conducted throughout the village at Ks'waan. These are significant finds as they are the first archaeologically recorded findings of abalone in a shell midden site within the heart of Gitxaała territory. The presence of abalone shells and shell fragments in the soil of our old villages indicates human use at or before the time of European arrival (Menzies 2015).

Contemporary Accounts of Long-standing Practice

Harvesting methods for bilhaa involved hand picking at low tide or use of a passive trap set at low tide and then harvested at the next low tide. This trap method involved the use of either sealskin or a flat, light-colored plank. The trap would be weighed down at the low tide level. As the water covered it, bilhaa would gather on the light-colored material. At the next low tide any bilhaa that stayed on the trap would be harvested.

The typical manner of picking bilhaa is at the low, low tides. It is *ha'wałks* (taboo) to pick bilhaa from in the water or under the water beyond what a person can normally reach scrambling along the beach (people call the shoreline "beach" in English, but these are fairly rocky, steep shorelines) or from a small canoe or skiff moving along the water's edge. A similar method of harvesting bilhaa is described for the Haida (Jones et al. 2004). In both cases the combination of technology and environmental conditions acts as a potential ecological limiting factor on harvesting. Techniques and tools could have been used to overharvest bilhaa, yet bilhaa were not overharvested until the development of DFO-regulated, market-oriented bilhaa fishing in 1972.

Sigidmnaanax (matriarchs) Agnes Shaw, Charlotte Brown, Violet Skog, and Janet Moody described in some detail the old ways of harvesting bilhaa; steaming the harvest on the beach in the sand with heated rocks, skunk cabbage leaves, and water; and then drying the cleaned meat in the sun or near a slow fire. Agnes and Charlotte describe harvesting bilhaa on the west coast of Banks Island. Violet, lamenting the loss of bilhaa, said, "Bilhaa was the first to go. We used to have lots. My mom used to dry them at Banks. Now we can't find anything. It's so hard to get the seafood now. Everything is just gone." Janet too describes harvesting bilhaa on Banks Island. Dried bilhaa was traded with people upriver for, among other things, moose meat, oolichan grease, and soapberries.

Like most women of their generation (in their late seventies to nineties), these women spent a great deal of time living and working in the hereditary territories. The annual cycle of food harvesting and preparation involved extensive periods at special resource harvest sites for seaweed, halibut, bilhaa, seal, deer, goat, salmon, and other foods. Charlotte described collecting seaweed as a child and a young woman with her family on Banks Island (at her uncle's and father's traditional site), where she also picked bilhaa: "May at Banks—we got seaweed, bilhaa—there was lots of it. They were too big to cook in the stove so we would dig in the sand and put leaves inside. Then we put hot rocks on top with a hole in the top. We'd pour in water and steam them. Then we'd hang them to dry after they were cooked. We used skunk cabbage leaves. After the fishing was done we'd stay and dry fish. Sometimes seven hundred fish. We'd hang them up and dry them. We got halibut woks [then sliced, dried fish] when we got seaweed. We would move into a small camp with just two houses to dry the halibut."

Bilhaa were easy to pick; there were so many that you could hear their shells hitting together. (Most of the older people that I have spoken with have commented, at one time or another, on the noise the bilhaa used to make before the K̲'amksiwa̲h harvesters reduced the local stock. The bilhaa would gather in large clumps, and the sound of their shells hitting one another was clearly audible.) Charlotte wasn't able to recall how many bilhaa her family harvested—"lots" was her comment. There was enough, at any rate, to have as a regular food item throughout the winter and to trade with people from the Skeena, Nass, and Kemano for goods such as soapberries and oolichan grease.

Sm'ooygit Matthew Hill explained to me in a conversation that a typical family group might harvest about five hundred pounds of bilhaa for the winter. A larger family would harvest more. Even more would be harvested if a yaawk was being prepared.

In an interview in February 2002 Sm'ooygit Jeffrey Spencer made the following comment about bilhaa harvesting and abundance and their importance as part of household food provisioning: "Bilhaa, there was really lots round here. No one bothered you if you catch a hundred pounds. Not anymore, they all go to the Chinese. In Vancouver I went to buy some sea cucumbers in Chinatown. I went to buy seven, thinking it would be maybe fifty dollars. For a seven-inch live one it was thirty-five dollars. That's our livelihood taken away from us. So now we just live on bologna and wieners. Bilhaa, we used to boil them and then string them. Hang them in the smokehouse. When you want to cook it, soak in salt water you get from the ocean. There was no such thing as a deep freeze or run out of power. Cockles and clams we did the same thing. We smoke seal, sea lion. Slice them up and smoke them. Salmon and seafood—that's how we survived."

Kenneth Innes, a contemporary resource harvester, highlights the lessons he has learned about bilhaa harvesting and the problems with the contemporary fishery: "Like with the Bilhaa. The Creator made the water only go down so far. So you can only harvest what you see. The commercial fishery dives for them and wiped them out. The sea urchins and goeducks will be the same. They can get at all of them if they dive."

The late Russell Lewis, who was an active resource harvester, had this to say:

RUSSELL LEWIS: My mom was really good at trading. I mean she was well known by the Gitxsans and the Nisga'as in the canneries and more mostly North Pacific. She did a lot of trading there. And she would trade bilhaa, seaweed, a whole bunch of stuff that she preserved here; that's what she did, what I remember anyways. So, they did a lot of trading with bilhaa.

AUTHOR: Did you know what she traded for, what did she get in return?

RUSSELL: Most of the things that I seen there was from up there, there was either, if you were going to the Nisga'a, you gotta get their grease or whatever, or the other one was soapberries, I remember soapberries, a lot of that, back then.

Bilhaa evokes strong meanings, strong feelings, and a deep attachment to place for Gitxaała. Methods of harvest continue to be transmitted through a community of practice. Youth are instructed in the principles of syt güülum goot; people visit their traditional harvesting sites; and our histories and songs are retold even in the face of the DFO closure of the bilhaa fishery.

Shutting Down the Fishery

The closure of the bilhaa fishery has had a significant impact upon Gitxaała people. Specifically it has resulted in the loss of a critical food resource, the loss of a critical trade item, and an increase of surveillance on aboriginal harvesters.

The sense of loss and desire is reflected in Elder and Sm'ooygit Jeffery Spencer's comments in a November 2001 interview: "Seaweed and bilhaa and . . . ooh, I want to talk about bilhaa—chew it in my mouth. I never taste that for a long time. [Laughter] Pretty hard to get. Don't allowed to get it. Don't allowed to get it. I just don't know why. I just don't know why."

In a separate interview Janet Moody commented, "It's . . . when the fisheries knew that bilhaa is abundant, they opened it, they got license, and like I said, they used divers, they went down and started picking them, and that's when they disappeared. Like I said, you can just stand there and you can hear them. . . . Sounds really nice, when they're walking like that. Today they're all gone. And to me, it's not our fault. It's not our fault, it's their own work. And we still do have a right to harvest that for our own use, cause we don't sell it. We eat it ourselves. And it's them that did harm on it. And now they're trying to punish us, and telling us not to get bilhaa, and that's wrong. It's our tradition, it was given to us. Our heavenly father gave us what kind of food to eat, what kind of medicine that we use with plants, he gave us how to survive, and it's the fisheries that's spoiling that, that's why it's gone from us."

Speaking to the perceptions of monitoring harassment, Russell Lewis said, "That's what's really hurting, myself; I can understand the species at risk thing, but you shouldn't go that far, it's not very good—just going out there myself now to try and do my harvest, I'm scared; who's watching me? I went over there to pick, and not even five minutes after I got off there, that boat come around. So I knew how they found us, I knew right away that they got the eye in the sky there. So it's not too much anybody can do, so . . . [Pause] It's really sad and me, when I go out to try and harvest any of my food, I'm wondering, is somebody there watching me? I know I've always been boarded, and searched, and that really hurts, when we're trying to harvest our own, for our traditional use, for our use only. I have a hard time, I have to meet with DFO, and . . . [Pause] It's hard for me to put it into words how I feel about them, because I have to work with them. I can understand the frustrations from our community onto me, because I get a lot of questions, 'Why are they [the DFO patrol vessel] tied here [to our dock]?' Well, we try to negotiate about that, we were successful in lowering that harassment or whatever you want to call it, the monitoring."

At the same time as Gitxaała community members perceive increased and excessive monitoring of their food harvesting practices, they also believe there is a lack of sufficient attention placed on monitoring commercial dive fishermen and recreational dive fishermen. On many occasions I have heard comments to the effect that enforcement against the large-scale illegal harvesting operations is insufficient and that excess enforcement appears to be applied to Gitxaała community harvesters. During my many visits to Gitxaała I too have observed DFO vessels in the nearby inlet and at the community dock more often during zero tides than at other times. Serendipitously I had the opportunity to confirm this from DFO enforcement officers in person.

While participating in a workshop on the oolichan fishery in Prince Rupert in March 2009 I had a chance to speak with DFO enforcement officials. During one of the breaks in the two-day workshop I outlined my observations to one of the officers. When I suggested that I would need access to the ship's log to see if my observations were correct, the officer said, "No need to do that. We always go out on the zero tides because that's when the local people are picking abalone." When I asked about enforcement of the dive fleet he said that there isn't the time or manpower to monitor the underwater fishery. "It's easy to see someone picking abalone on a zero tide—it's a lot harder to catch a diver," he explained. It would seem that community sentiment is correct: DFO is focusing on aboriginal harvesters rather than targeting the commercial and illegal dive fishermen who work without regard to zero tides.

Returning to a Sustainable Fishery

Despite DFO surveillance, bilhaa continues to be illegally harvested by non-Gitxaała people, to the detriment of both Gitxaała and bilhaa. In Gitxaała we have contained our own harvests within the context of our own authority and jurisdiction. However, that is insufficient as long as the illegal non-Gitxaała fishing persists. There is a solution with the potential to benefit Gitxaała and bilhaa: returning management control to Gitxaała under our traditional system of harvest and governance. As my colleague Caroline Butler and I have documented elsewhere, "Gitxaala people have been taught by their Elders to take only what they need, not to overexploit the natural resources. 'Take what you need' was in fact the standard response in reply to questions about how to use the resources sustainably, and what the Elders taught them about harvesting" (Menzies and Butler 2007, 455–56). Across the Hecate Straits on Haida Gwaii (Queen Charlotte Islands), the Haida and their non-Haida neighbors have been able to establish control over bilhaa in Gwaii Haanas (the national park in the southern islands), drawing upon the powers of Parks Canada and Haida authority and jurisdiction over their traditional territory (Jones et al. 2004) by establishing a co-management regime.

By drawing upon Gitxaała resource harvesting principles and our associated harvesting practices and techniques, a sustainable bilhaa fishery is possible. The Haida comanagement model is one path that could be followed. In Gitxaała, however, hereditary leaders and community members prefer to manage under our own authority and jurisdiction. Linking new fishery science knowledge with the Gitxaała house governance and the principle of syt güülum goot, a revived and sustainable bilhaa fishery is possible in laxyuup Gitxaała.

8

Hoon

Salmon

I must have been twelve or thirteen the first time I saw an old stone
fish trap. It was late July, warm, crisp blue skies. I was playing around
on the water at the head of a small cove, marking the time until the
commercial seine fishing would begin. Drifting along with the tide, I
was watching coho salmon swimming below me illuminated by the
bright sun. Then I saw the walls of stone on the ocean floor. I was cap-
tivated by the intricacies of the stonework, a fascination that has stayed
with me for more than three decades. Back on my father's fishing boat
I asked him about the stone walls in the water. "That," he said, "that's
an old fish trap. They used to drag seine here."

There is a common misperception that prior to the arrival of the
K̲'amksiw̲ah the natural world was pristine and untouched. Indigenous
peoples on the Northwest Coast were thought to have lived opportunistically on the bounty of nature. While we do know that, though
abundant, these resources were not guaranteed (Suttles 1987), the idea
that our Indigenous ancestors had no significant impact on the environment (unless of course they were massacring Pleistocene megafau-
na; for an informed discussion of this issue, see Kelly and Prasciunas
2007) is a persistent Euro-American myth.

This chapter challenges the myth of the pristine and untouched natural world. My challenge may not prove the case, but through my reflections, considerations, and speculations I wish to challenge readers
to consider that the world that the K̲'amksiw̲ah entered in the late

1700s was no "natural" world but the outcome of a deliberate and direct human-environment interaction over millennia.

I grew up working on a salmon seiner skippered by my father. I spent my summers with him on the boat and much of my time in the winter after school working alongside him in gear lockers and engine rooms, doing the tasks one does to keep a large wooden boat afloat and ready to fish. In the summer we traveled and fished throughout the north coast. The area of my childhood travels mirrors, to a large extent, if imperfectly, the traditional territory of my Gitxaała ancestors. I felt connected to this place and people through the stories my father told me, and the places where we fished.

My first experience of seeing a stone trap has stayed with me. It was a captivating sight for a young boy. But even as an adult the often intensely complex construction is impressive. One cannot leave a stone trap site without considering the implications of human labor in the environment. I grew up with stories of my great grandfather's fishing camp in K'moda. Yet seeing the curved walls of stone in the water made me think quite differently about what might actually be involved in building these structures. As noted in the three accounts below, some significant quantity of labor is required to construct, maintain, and then operate fisheries using stone trap gear.

In the 1970s and early 1980s I was very much involved in salmon enhancement projects and discussions. As a professional researcher in the 1990s I was involved in watershed restoration projects and conducting oral history research into traditional management practices that could be deployed in the present. Throughout these experiences I started to note a similarity between the ancient practices described to me and inscribed within the creeks and shorelines of Gitxaała territory and the contemporary scientific models of enhancement and restoration.

Community harvesters I interviewed framed creekscaping and harvesting techniques in terms of relations between humans and nonhuman social beings. That is, one's behavior is regulated by one's social relations, which are understood as kin-like (see, for example, Langdon 2006). This implies and requires a structure of obligation and reciprocity. One learns this firsthand through experience on the water and land. But these lessons are also heard and reinforced in the oral histories of

Gitxaała people, some of which have been recorded over the past century and a half (recall the story of Txemsum and his wife, the Princess of the Salmon, in chapter 5).

The stone fish traps and associated Indigenous practices discussed in this chapter document some of what is actually done in terms of creekscaping and fishing techniques. These practices have implications for purposeful conservation management practices. It is useful to remind ourselves that the extension of Canadian law into aboriginal fisheries and land management practices has involved an explicit attempt to disrupt and displace aboriginal practices (Harris 2008). Thus since the 1880s Gitxaała fisheries practices were essentially criminalized and the fisheries transformed into a so-called food fishery for Indians (which First Nations are allowed to harvest for social and ceremonial purposes) and a commercial fishery for "everyone" (in which the sale of fish for economic benefit is permitted).

When one compares the catch data over the past 150 or so years with the estimates of pre-$\underline{K}$'amksiw$\underline{a}$h harvest levels, the numbers are roughly equivalent over several millennia (Glavin 1996). As Michael Kew (1989, 180) notes, "The Indian salmon fishery stands as a prime example of high utilization and dependence by humans over a long period of time with no depletion of the resource." Put another way: the commercial and aboriginal fisheries caught about the same amount of fish, but in 150 years of the commercial fishery salmon have been pushed to a dangerously low level. What happened? Very likely the criminalization of aboriginal creekscaping and fisheries practices played a significant role in undermining the health of salmon stocks in BC (Harris 2008; Menzies and Butler 2007).

Prior to the extension of the Canadian Fisheries Act to British Columbia in the 1880s Gitxaała people actively managed and shaped creeks and associated spawning channels, increasing spawning areas by modifying the watercourse. In addition they managed harvesting by controlling the number of salmon entering the spawning channels. All of these actions had the effect of stabilizing the amount of salmon available for Gitxaała harvesting.

Gitxaała management practices were essentially a form of Keynesian management. That is, the human interaction with the environment cut off the high peaks and low valleys of fish runs to generate a stable and reliable supply of fish. Because of the reproductive strategy of salmon (r-selection: that is, a high number of offspring from low parental investment) the fish can react quickly to changes in their environment. This strategy also allows for the augmentation of runs beyond the potential capacity of spawning grounds. As a side consequence it provides surplus fish that can be harvested without affecting the long-term sustainability of the fish stock. This is a classic tenet of contemporary salmon management practices, and it does appear to have been a successful part of Indigenous salmon management prior to the criminalization of Indigenous practices in the late 1800s.

The customary fishing methods of Northwest Coast First Nations comprise a highly varied and refined assemblage of technologies, reflecting millennia of development and innovations. These fishing technologies and gears were designed with micro-ecological factors in mind: tides, eddies, and other water features; seasonal considerations; and the behavior of target species. The method and gear used at a particular site were selected according to multiple factors to improve efficiency without destroying fish stocks for future use. These highly specialized technologies allowed for sustained yields of salmon, providing adequate food supplies for many First Nations for thousands of years (Berringer 1982; Newell 1993; Stewart 1977).

Traditional fishing gears included gaffs, clubs, traps, weirs, trolling hooks, drag seines, gill nets, tidal traps, spears, dip nets, hooks on lines, and fish rakes (McDonald 1991). Each of these gears was associated with particular fishing sites, species, and seasons. The following case studies explore the interconnection between locally appropriate gear types, Indigenous history and knowledge systems related to each fishing site, and the implications of all this for the idea of cultivating salmon. Each account offers a unique vantage point from which to consider the specific question at hand.

K'moda is a location that figures prominently within my own family's history. It is the site of one of the first canneries on the north coast and a site of ancient conflict between the northern invaders and Gitxaała and their Gitga'ata cousins. A stream named Kxooyax also figures in the history of early encounters with K̲'amksiwa̲h; here Capt. James

Colnett's crew decided to tear apart a portion of the stone fish trap. But this is also where Gitxaała people learned an early lesson about treating salmon with respect and the cost of not doing so. It is a place where K̲'amksiwa̲h laws came into conflict with Gitxaała laws over the allocation of fishing rights. Kxenk'aa'wen (Place of Fishing Trap) stands out as a place with an amazing complex of stone traps; in fact the place-name is a direct reference to the special nature of the local stone fish traps. K̲'amksiwa̲h also encountered Gitxaała people here early in their commercial trading ventures along this coast. More important, Kxenk'aa'wen is a place where people live and have lived for millennia harvesting a multitude of resources, not least of which are salmon in the unique traps the place is named after.

Fishing at K'moda

K'moda is a river and lake system at the head of Lowe Inlet within Gitxaała territory. This is the traditional territory of Sm'ooygit He:l. Over the past century and a half this place has been at the center of significant social transformations. This is also the place at the heart of many of the stories that my father would tell me about my great-grandfather Edward Gamble and my uncle Russell Gamble. I have been fortunate to have had the opportunity to visit this place many times. One notable trip stands out.

As I described in chapter 4, I organized a research trip with my cousin Teddy Gamble, who took us to Lowe Inlet on his gillnetter. We were joined on this trip by Sm'ooygit He:l (Russell Gamble), my father, my sons, and my colleague Caroline Butler. Being able to listen to my father and uncle speak about this place and their recollections of fishing and the people who once lived there shapes my understanding in ways that my written words may not be able to convey. When I return to this place I still see them there on the beach, talking. My memory of this trip has transformed the abstract landscape into a social space through which my family has passed and to which it retains an important connection. Thus while I write about the fish trap and the history of salmon fisheries and management I do so aware of the larger social world within which this place is more than just a place to catch fish.

In the late 1880s one the earliest salmon canneries in BC was established here. Employing local Gitga'ata and Gitxaała community members the cannery operated for several decades spanning the late nineteenth and early twentieth century. Coastal steamers made regular stops here on the Inside Passage route from Vancouver to Alaska. The Harriman expedition, notable for the number of Indigenous objects they removed without permission and donated to U.S. museums, passed through here on its way north to Alaska in 1899. Photographer Edward Curtis took a few pictures of the area while other scientists onboard collected plant samples. The census taker recorded in his personal journal his trials and tribulations in attempting to take census data during his visit in 1881 to the Gitxaała houses at the mouth of the K'moda.

Records of customary use and commercial trade by a Gitxaała sm'ooygit are inscribed in the Canadian Sessional Papers.[1] One, dated 1890, states, "The chief at Lowe's Inlet, assisted by his sons, caught and sold to two canneries on the Skeena River forty thousand fish, at an average of seven and eight cents each."[2] Oral accounts describe the close interconnection between customary use in the area and the development of a local Gitxaała and Gitga'ata labor force that caught and processed salmon in the Lowe Inlet cannery.

Some find the combination of traditional and commercial fisheries practices to be either a contradiction in terms or evidence of acculturation. However, this is far from the case for Indigenous fisheries along the west coast of Canada. Those who believe that aboriginal fisheries were always subsistence endeavors or just for food are mistaken. This colonial misconception underlies a great many historical and contemporary ruminations on aboriginal fisheries. In point of fact Gitxaała harvesters have always harvested for domestic consumption, gift exchange, and exchange for benefit. The development of the K'amksiwah commercial salmon fishery, especially in its early decades, fit well within the entrepreneurial culture of Gitxaała and neighboring Indigenous communities.

For generations K'moda has been the house territory of the leading sm'ooygit from Gitxaała, Sm'ooygit He:l. The late Sm'ooygit He:l (Russell Gamble) explained that during the middle of the twentieth century K'moda was occupied by the chief and house group from late spring through early fall. Resources gathered included mountain goats, deer, a range of different berries, bark, clams and cockles, seals, and, of course, salmon and other fish. Elders who were young children during the early twentieth century recall the life of the campsite during the leadership of Sm'ooygit Seax/He:l (Edward Gamble), nephew and heir of Ts'ibasaa. Edward Gamble was the named hereditary chief who held this site in the decades prior to his heir, Russell Gamble.

Over the course of the twentieth century the fishing patterns at K'moda evolved from customary harvesting for consumption and exchange for benefit (up to about 1880), to a period of intense industrial harvesting coexisting with customary harvesting (1880–1930), to locally controlled drag seining (1930–67), and finally, to less intensive, occasional customary harvest using gill nets (1967 to present). In what follows I describe the key aspects of the customary techniques of fish harvesting, using data from site visits to K'moda with Sm'ooygit He:l (see chapter 4) and interviews with Gitxaała elders and community members who actively use or have used this place for the harvest of fish and other resources.

Three key customary fishing techniques have been deployed at K'moda: gaffs, stone tidal traps, and drag seines (Menzies and Butler 2007). Up until the late 1800s fishing with gaffs and stone traps was the key technique for harvesting salmon. Coincident with the development of the industrial salmon canning fishery Gitxaała fishers switched to drag seining. This innovation accommodated the reduction in the labor force caused by the waves of disease and dislocation brought by invasive non-Indigenous humans.

Stone traps can be found throughout the Northwest Coast region (see, for example, Langdon 2006; Stewart 1977). Traps were typically located near streams and rivers where migrating salmon traveled as they returned to spawn in the fall. Traps consisted of a series of stones arranged in a semicircular design. Boulders and stones were stacked upon each other. No mortar was used to hold the stones together; instead careful selection and placement of the stones was required. In this way the wall of stones would remain upright in rough weather and throughout vigorous tidal action. Stone traps were used by house groups, relying on collaborative labor under the guidance of the house leader.

Stone fishing traps use the principle of tidal drift to catch fish. Salmon gather near the mouth of their birth river or stream in preparation to spawn. When the water is deep enough, the salmon enter the river system and swim upstream. As the tide comes in, the salmon are pushed toward the shore and the waiting trap. When the tide recedes, the salmon move downstream, away from the shore. As they swim away from the shore with the current they become trapped by the wall of stones. Fishers would position themselves along the wall as the tide dropped and splash the water to keep the fish from swimming out before the water was lower than the wall.

The K'moda stone trap is located in a small cove near, but not in or across, the opening of the creek. Its design, like all stone fishing traps, uses tidal drift to capture fish. Elders report that the number of salmon returning to spawn in creeks and streams was so vast that a trap located at the beach, anywhere close to a stream would provide a rich harvest.

Trap placement, however, typically takes advantage of the micro movements of local currents; this technology is not simply placed near or in a creek mouth. At K'moda the trap is located to the north of the creek's actual mouth. During our observations of tidal patterns we noted that at about three-quarter ebb a back eddy formed, which acted as a great broom sweeping the fish into the belly of the trap. Then, as the tide receded, the current dropped the fish behind the trap's wall, allowing the fishers to select those fish that were required for processing that day.

Streamscaping at Kxooyax

Kxooyax is a stream and lake system located on the southeastern shore of Banks Island. This ancient fishing site is the territory of Gilasgamgan, Laskiik. It has been a site of significant Gitxaała fisheries prior to, at, and well past the point of initial encounter with Europeans.

James Colnett, captain of the vessel *Prince of Wales*, made the first known European record of this trap in October 1787. Colnett's crew fished here without permission from the local title holder and dismantled a portion of the trap: "The Wire that was fixed in the Run was to prevent the fish from getting too hastily up as well as down, & some of our people out of pity for the sickly fish above broke part of the wire down by which means the fish had a free passage up & when the run increased nothing to stop them" (Galois 2004, 157).[3] Colnett's inability to recognize the existing Indigenous regulations and customs related to use of local resources ultimately resulted in conflict between his crew and Gitxaała people. After Colnett's early account of Kxooyax this place enters the official Euro-Canadian historical record via the assignment of a reserve for Gitxaała and the licensing of fishing rights by the Canadian government.

Following a meeting with Gitxaała hereditary leaders at K'moda in July 1891, Indian Reserve Commissioner Peter O'Reilly agreed to establish Indian Reserve 12, Ks-or-yet (variant of Kxooyax), for Gitxaała. He described the reserve as composed of twenty-eight acres and "situated on the eastern shore of Banks Island, about four mile north of Gale Point."[4] F. A. Devereux surveyed the reserve in May 1892 and noted the presence of an "Indian house" within its boundary.[5]

In 1911 the Canadian government assigned the commercial drag seine fishing rights to BC Packers (License No. 18, Bare Bay).[6] The majority of these drag seine licenses were normally operated by the Indigenous title holder, the hereditary leader who would customarily be considered the individual with rights to use and governance over such places. The assignment of fishing rights to nonaboriginal fishing companies were not without problems. In 1890, for example, Sm'ooygit Seax (here written as Chief Shukes) advised a cannery manager operating near his territory to stop fishing. Seax's enactment of his authority and jurisdiction is recorded in a letter from M. K. Morrison, fishery guardian, to Thomas Mowat, inspector of fisheries:

I was down to Low's Inlet and around Banks Island where I found considerable trouble between the Low's Inlet Canning people and the Indians, the cause I will try and make clear to you. Part of Low's Inlet is an Indian Reserve (Kitk-a-thla Tribe), the Cannery is not on the Reserve where the fish is caught inside the Reserve line salt water, but close to the falls the same has to be hauled on Indian reserve below high water mark—Chef Shukes forbid the Cannery people to fish, if they did he and his young men would cut their nets. . . . I went to Shukes and he told me as follows: Judge O'Reilly gave this land and water to my people, I do not want any Whitemen to fish here please tell your chief I have fished at Low's Inlet for 8 years, it is the principal support of myself and people. . . . The Indians on Banks Island told the Captain of the "Murrial" if he put out a seine to fish in their water he would be shot, he did not do it had not men enough.[7]

The cannery licensing system also interfered with Gitxaała customary practices by preferentially allocating licenses to community members in ways that were not in accord with traditional practices. Thus, on September 30, 1915, a petition of complaint was submitted to the Royal Commission on Indian Affairs regarding the process of assigning fishing rights at Kxooyax:

> There is a salmon creek running on Eastside of Banks Island below Bare Hill called in our language K'Oyaht [a variant of Kxooyax] and from immemorial our forefathers in our family own it and claim it as their own, and it is from where they generally obtain their living . . . but, some years ago another man of different family butt in and troubling us by taking advantage of us in taking away that salmon creek from us, and we've pressed out by him. He has been running that creek since for Lowe Inlet Cannery . . . and now we want to take it back from him through you by recognizing it to us. It was reserved to our family by or through the late Indian Agent. . . . This man's name who took that place away from us is Alfred Robinson also of Kitkatla, B.C. He has no right to claim that place and salmon creek other than us. We'll mention the names of only four of our forefathers herewith who own that place mentioned above from immemorial . . . Milsh, Haqulockgamlahap, Dwilthlagianat and Lthgooshamun. . . . We are their descendants and therefore we have right to run that salmon creek ourselves for that cannery. . . . We want to be allowed to get our own drag seine license for that salmon creek for next season.[8]

Echoes of these disagreements reverberate in the present.

My own first visit to this place, nearly two centuries later, was in the 1970s while fishing with my father. This is the same area where I first saw a stone trap (as described earlier). Since the late 1990s I have revisited this place several times in order to record and observe the stone trap complex in greater detail. The stone trap complex at Kxooyax differs significantly from the K'moda trap. Whereas the K'moda trap adjoins the stream mouth, at Kxooyax the trap complex is located in the creek mouth and entrance channel.

At least eight individual rock alignment features and three retaining pool features are identifiable along both sides of the creek extending over an area of approximately 430 meters in length and ranging in elevation from a low of 2.45 meters below the current barnacle line to 0.5 meters above the barnacle line. The longest border alignment is 81 meters and is located in the center of the stream in a V-shaped formation that substantially alters the stream flow. Four shorter linear features are present along the lower reaches of the southern stream bank running nearly perpendicular to the stream. These features run parallel to each other but do not match up with similar features on the northern stream bank. A distinct 50-meter-long arc-shaped boulder alignment follows the stream flow, in contrast to the four linear features on the southern shoreline. The alignment located closest to the stream outlet extends all the way across the stream channel. This particular feature is visible only at low-low tide. The lower reaches of Kxooyax Stream have been extensively modified and engineered to facilitate access to the salmon fishery. The complexity and extent of the features represent a significant intergenerational commitment in securing access and managing the use of salmon at this place. The location of a canoe run along the north side of the stream mouth (near the Indian house documented by Devereux) further demonstrates the extent of human use of this area.

There is no way Kxooyax can be thought of as a "natural" space; it is totally creekscaped. The path of the stream—from the high-tide mark to the lowest low-tide mark—shows clear evidence of human modification. Deep V-shaped stone structures provide access points for gaffing and dip-netting salmon. Holding pools along the sides of the stream in the upper reaches of the tidal area allowed for live storage and selective removal of fish according to processing and consumption needs. This is a human-designed space dedicated to the harvesting of salmon.

Kxenk'aa'wen (Place of Special Trap)

Kxenk'aa'wen, also known as Bonilla Arm, is an inlet on the west coast of Banks Island noted for, among other things, its seaweed, seals, fish, and a range of productive salmon streams. This is an ancient place within the Gitxaała world, with histories linking contemporary title holders back beyond the ken of time. The very name, Kxenk'aa'wen, can be translated as Place of Special Trap. Indeed there is a special and amazing example of stone fish traps here. Along one side of the inlet, stretching for a full kilometer, is a complex of stone traps the like of which is seldom observed along BC's coast. (See Smethurst 2014 for an extensive analysis of these traps and associated human use and occupancy.)

Kxenk'aa'wen is one of the places the Gitxaała people first met the K̲'amksiwa̱h. Gitxaała people fishing halibut off Lax t'xal (Bonilla Island) sighted a strange being floating offshore. "The greatest number [of Gitxaała people] would gather on the west coast of Banks Island, and Bonilla Island (lax t'xal). Here over a large area they would fish for halibut. One day these people set out as usual for their fishing each choosing a locality and all being very close to one another, in case of sudden danger. Then the chief Sabaan and his slave went the furthest out to sea to get more halibut then [*sic*] the rest. All were busy engaged in fishing and suddenly as if coming from nowhere, there appeared a huge being with many wings and no noise, it came so suddenly among the people that they were barely able to pull up their anchors and escape" (Beynon notebook, 1955–56, CMC). Upon investigation Sabaan realized it was a vessel with sails, not wings, and strange people onboard, not a supernatural being.

The academic literature concerning these first encounters distills the various Gitxaała narratives into a singular event in which Colnett met with Gitxaała at Ks'waan (Calamity Bay; discussed earlier in relation to Kxooyax [Galois 2004]). However, an alternative understanding, and one that is more in keeping with Gitxaała perspectives, is that these historical narratives relate a series of encounters between Gitxaała and K̲'amksiwa̱h peoples. Colnett was not alone in traveling through these waters. At least a half-dozen ships are known to have been here around the time of Colnett's voyage. Thus the K̲'amksiwa̱h academics writing about this issue have overlooked the possibility that variations in this story may in fact be evidence of different first encounters rather than errors of memory and discursive flourishes on the part of latter-day storytellers.

The contemporary title holders, Inta 'we walp and Kaymt Kwa', exercise rights and responsibilities for this place whose history goes back long before the K̲'amksiwa̲h drifted up on these coasts. Both men continue to this day to live on and from the products of their labor in this place. This unique place has a long history of interconnected resource use within which salmon is a critical, but not exclusive, object of harvest.

Given the nature of the fish traps, how they are laid out along the shoreline, their shape, and their placement in relation to local streams, the target species were likely pink and dog salmon. Unlike sockeye, these two salmon species travel close to shore in dense schools. (Sockeye tend to run farther off the beach.) Pink and dog salmon are thus particularly amenable to harvest using large half-moon-shaped stone barricades. Sockeye, another prime target species, is more likely harvested on its way up the stream mouth, given its different traveling behavior. Thus at Kxooyax, which is a sockeye stream, the stone traps are located within the creek. In Kxenk'aa'wen the stone traps are located along the shoreline where they can more effectively intercept pink and dog salmon (though there are significant sockeye runs here as well).

With the development of the industrial commercial salmon fishery in the late 1800s came changes in fishing techniques and gear types even as the cultural values of Gitxaała remained consistent with the ancestors (Menzies and Butler 2008). In Kxenk'aa'wen a shift occurred away from the use of stone and wooden traps to cotton drag seines and then, in the mid-twentieth century, to seines and gill nets operated from motorized vessels. The operators of the new gear types remained the traditional title holders and members of their house groups.

The exact date of the transition from stone traps to drag seines is not clear from either the oral history or the documentary record. It is conceivable that the transition predated K̲'amksiwa̲h arrival, occurred at the moment K̲'amksiwa̲h first arrived (early maritime traders used drag seines in Gitxaała territory to harvest fish for food), or occurred later in the nineteenth century with the emergence of the industrial commercial fishery. Gitxaała people had the knowledge and the capacity to produce nettle twine nets that could have been used as drag seines prior to the arrival of marine traders using seines. Coast Salish fishers in the Fraser River estuary and surrounding areas used large stationary nets to trap salmon (see, for example, Kew 1989; Suttles 1987). Thus the leap from drag seines is not significant conceptually for experienced coastal fishermen like the Gitxaała. However, given that the catching capacity of the traps appears to be more than sufficient for the supply of labor available prior to contact, it is also possible that there was no reason to shift technology until the new diseases brought by K̲'amksiwa̲h (smallpox, measles, flu) devastated coastal communities in one wave of death after another (Boyd 1999; Campbell 2005). What is clear is that the customary laws of access and proprietorship governing these fishing sites date well before K̲'amksiwa̲h arrival and have continued into the present.

Changes in technique and gear type have implications for labor deployment. Fishing with stone traps would require a community effort in which intergenerational labor would be deployed and harvesting and processing would be coordinated. Shifting to drag seining for the commercial fishery would sever the coordination between harvesting and processing. Aside from processing related to household consumption and trade, the majority of processing would be shifted out of community control into industrial fish processing plants. Furthermore the labor requirement would be reduced as the operation of a drag seine requires at most a dozen people. The harvested fish would be immediately loaded onto a tender boat and then transported to the fish processing plant. Household fish processing would likely drop to about five hundred to one thousand fish per household given that most production of fish for economic benefit had been redirected to the industrial fish processing plants rather than held and processed within community processing facilities (i.e., local smokehouses).

Sigyidm hana̲'a̲ Agnes Shaw and Charlotte Brown grew up in Kxenk'aa'wen. In a series of interviews and conversations they described their experience growing up and living in their father's clan territory in the early twentieth century. Their father, William Lewis, and his brother, James, were members of the Gispuwada (blackfish) house group. Agnes comments, "When my dad get some seal, and then he'd call my grandfather [Samuel Wise Lewis] up, his father. And that was Albert Argyle's house, where my dad stayed, in Kxenk'aa'wen, and then when he [Albert] died, then my dad moved in into his house" (July 4, 2005). Agnes and Charlotte describe an annual cycle that began in May with the seaweed and halibut harvest and finished in the late fall, when the last salmon was put up in the big smokehouse located near their homes at Kxenk'aa'wen. A short list of resources harvested includes abalone, seal, sea lion, halibut, deer, and several species of berries. The people also maintained a garden out on Lax t'xal that was noted for its large white potatoes.

Agnes and Charlotte explained that they would stay out at Banks after finishing the commercial drag seine fishery to put up their own fish. "There's a big smokehouse in Bonilla Arm. Four women in that big smokehouse. They divided it into four sections for those four ladies. One [section] for each lady" (Agnes Shaw, March 10, 2005). Charlotte estimated that the "women put up about seven hundred fish each for their households" (December 14, 2001). Agnes described the process: "We would dry the fish, my mom and me. Hundreds of fish in the big smokehouse. When they were dry, we put them higher up, to make them really dry. In the winter to eat them, we soak it overnight to get the salt out and then boil it. We did that for halibut too. Seal we would dry it really dry, sea lion too." (February 11, 2002).

Charlotte recalled drag seining in the early part of the twentieth century: "We were drag seining when Albert Argyle was alive. He was the owner of the river before, Killerwhale Clan. Last time we drag seined when I was small. They went into the salt lake and were fishing inside it. They got the boat in on a strong tide" (December 14, 2001).

Agnes has this to say about early drag seining: "I can just remember. It was so good what those guys used to do. And then, when the boat ran along the shore to Gushi'algun, and we'd ride along, we were on there with all the kids. After a while near the rapids [sxr'adzlaasen, salt water rapids created by the tide] these guys would get out and pull their canoes along the shore line [i.e., on foot], and then we'd pull the boat along to fish in the inlet by drag seine. And up by the tree line, that's where we'd sit, me and the rest of the ladies. And these ladies would get ready with their containers, empty cans, and then they'd spear crabs. I really wonder what that area is like today, whether there's lots of crabs there now. They'd build a big fire there. At twelve o'clock they'd [the men] come back and we'd all eat down the beach, they [the women] would build a fire and boil crabs. It was so good, what those people used to do" (July 4, 2005).

The contemporary title holders continue to live on resources harvested in their Kxenk'aa'wen territories. They still spend time in their territory, though likely not as much time as during Agnes and Charlotte's youth. Salmon fishing now occurs with the use of gill nets, which can be fixed in place or drifting. Whereas the stone traps required several households working together and the drag seines at least a dozen people to operate, gill nets need only one or two people in a small skiff (twelve to eighteen feet in length) or a commercial gillnetter (thirty-five to forty feet in length). In a small vessel with an outboard motor harvesters can selectively access their traditional territory and return home the same day without having to camp overnight. Nonetheless harvesters do remain on site for periods of time depending upon the particular resources they are harvesting. Despite changes in time spent in the territory and techniques used for harvesting, the customary protocols governing ownership and access still pertain.

Laxyuup Gitxaała and the Cultivation of Salmon

These examples of customary fishing sties, and their attendant human-modified environments, provide a backdrop to my contention that Gitxaała people purposefully managed salmon stocks. At each of these places fishing techniques relied upon similar principles of regulating who could fish, when they could fish, and how much fish would be taken. While the introduction of drag seine gear to Gitxaała territory is more recent than the stone trap or gaff fishing, it does have historical antecedents in north coast Indigenous fishing techniques. Nets of various sorts, including encircling seine-type nets, have been used for millennia by Indigenous fishers. Gear selection has been based on the particular ecological conditions at a site and the social dynamics of the community actively engaged in fishing the site. It should be pointed out that a variety of gears are employed not only across different sites but even at the same site. Thus fishers vary their harvesting techniques according to the time of year, local weather conditions and fish availability, and targeted species.

K'moda is a highly productive salmon watershed that, since the government's removal of Gitxaała engagement, has seen a marked decline in fish stocks. There are of course many factors to take into consideration, but the role of Gitxaała title holders in the health and well-being of salmon resources should not be overlooked. Stories relate how Edward Gamble would survey the stream above the tidal falls and direct young members of his household and crew as they cleared and structured the watercourse. The fish trap near the mouth of the creek was designed to take advantage of local tidal currents. The fishery at the falls allowed for selective removal of fish (Menzies and Butler 2007).

At Kxooyax the major modification of the creek above and below the high-tide line reflects the intensive investment of human labor power. This site remains a customary harvesting site. (In fact several times while we were there our crew set a net to harvest salmon for our own consumption.) Side pools and V-shaped structures point to techniques of fish harvesting that allowed effective removal of fish from the stream. In interviews with hereditary leaders and active resource harvesters we hear over and over accounts of active management of the fish.

Kxenk'aa'wen is notable for the large and expansive set of traps that cover nearly a kilometer of the intertidal zone. This is a system of multiple pink, chum, and sockeye salmon runs. Each species requires a somewhat different harvesting approach, and evidence in the material remains documents a diversity of harvesting techniques. This area remains a key traditional territory from which the local title holders harvest a range of marine resources.

A critical aspect of these Gitxaała fishing techniques is the ability to avoid or to release unharmed nontarget species. One of the problems encountered in the contemporary industrial fishery is the mix of stock. The fleet encounters a mass of fish that can include several species, spawners from a variety of creeks within the same species, and juveniles. Traditionally the industrial gears have found it difficult to release nontarget species without stress or damage. When it was discovered in 1997 that coho stocks in the Fraser and Skeena river systems had drastically declined, the fleet was required to release coho live at specific times and in particular areas (see Copes 1998). The stress on the fish during harvest required that they had to be individually resuscitated in "revival boxes" of fresh, flowing seawater before release. Selectivity, both of species and of particular spawning runs, continues to be an issue for commercial salmon harvesters. The priority of weak stock management to preserve biodiversity obligates the DFO to manage according to the weakest run of spawners in a system. If harvesters cannot identify and avoid salmon from a particular creek that has been identified as weak, then an entire fishery can be reduced or closed. When harvesting occurs at the mouth of a creek, the harvester knows exactly which spawning population is being targeted. Harvesting at close range ensures that the fisher can target a particular species (spring salmon rather than coho, etc.) or size of fish.

Similarly stone traps are located at or near the mouths of creeks. As I documented earlier, harvesting was regulated based on the house leader's observation of spawner abundance, and a specific ratio of harvest was maintained to prevent overly pressuring one run of fish. The trap functions to corral the fish into a small pond of water, and they are then removed by harvesters. The fishers can select by species and age at this point and leave the nontarget or juvenile fish to escape the trap as the tide rises. The drag seine, being very close in function to the stone trap, is selective on the same bases.

Gitxaała technologies are also supported by social relations, which guide and control their use. Whereas the K'amksiwah fishery was driven by capitalist market forces and catching efficiency, Gitxaała fishing techniques and approaches have been regulated by community-based use and harvesting principles within a cultural framework that treats salmon as a relative and a social being deserving of respect.

This chapter (and this book) began with the assumption that purposeful human-environment interactions are not the sole prerogative of late capitalist society. Of course this is not a new or startling assertion. There is empirical evidence for many disastrous human-environment interactions. Discussions of beneficial and positive outcomes, however, seems to me to be few and far between.

My experience growing up on the north coast of BC, my time working with my father on his fishing boat, and my trips to Gitxaała and through Gitxaała territory led me to question the idea that there was no intent or design behind all of that human labor that my ancestors gave to our traditional territory. There is more to do, more to say, more to consider, as this argument is advanced. Nonetheless, based on all that I have seen, it seems that the environment that forms Gitxaała territory was shaped by millennia of human practices and behaviors. It was not and is not pristine wilderness on which nature wrote her own story. Laxyuup Gitxaała is thus the outcome of millennia of inter-action, purposeful intervention, and human disturbance; this fact is what makes it the place it is today.

Conclusion

This book, this story is about core Gitxaała values and Gitxaała social institutions: names, governance, place (laxyuup), and history. This is what provides the intellectual and cultural framework that guides a Gitxaała way of being, a way of being that is grounded in the laxyuup—the place that Gitxaała call home. Everyday practices arise from direct engagement with the laxyuup. The story that I have told begins with the core values and then explores the ways these values are played out through the practice of fishing. Telling stories about catching fish, sharing fish, and eating fish is central to one core enactment of being Gitxaała.

Names of individuals and peoples, places, and regions are decisive political interventions. Whether the arena is that of inter-Indigenous conflict (recall the discussion on the use of Southern Tsimshian) or attempted colonial erasures by settlers who rename our laxyuup with English or Spanish names, names are important. Names root people and places in history and determine who can govern; therefore governance is tied to place through history. This is manifested in actions mundane (such as the simple act of catching a fish) and ritualized (such as distributing oolichan grease at a feast).

Being Gitxaała is thus a process that involves knowing both where one is from (in terms of place and socially as a person) and who one is (in terms of relations to other social beings). This is an entwined, spatially and temporally rooted ontology. Laws, history, and governance are all tied to history, place, and person. To be Gitxaała is to understand oneself as enmeshed within a community of relationships with people (understood broadly as human and nonhuman) and with a storied sense of place.

In this book I have explored how being Gitxaała is enacted through community practices of fisheries. I have reviewed the nature and extent of fisheries practices historically and today. Fish harvesting is a central aspect of Gitxaała practice. This book documents the broad extent of Gitxaała's resource harvesting, and the three case studies focus on abalone, herring, and salmon. Each highlights a particular feature and experience of being Gitxaała.

I discussed abalone as a culturally important species and the devastating effects of an uncontrolled harvest by K̲'amksiwa̲h fishers. The problem was the intrusion of an ill-conceived bio-economic model of resource management combined with an unrestrained market-oriented commercial fishery. In contrast, our data document an ancient and long-standing practice among Gitxaała of sustainable harvest.

Over the course of the colonial experience Indigenous resource utilization has been constrained and restricted. The case of herring demonstrates how the use of one resource narrowed over the course of a century. Utilization shifted from ancient times to the present: in the past herring was consumed whole and in quantities equivalent to that of salmon; today only the roe is consumed. The case illuminates the consequences of pathogenic colonialism combined with economic transition; that is, disease, death, and capitalism operating in concert created conditions that narrowed the utilization of herring.

The case study of salmon fishing documents the role of Indigenous husbandry of natural resources and the continuing importance of salmon as an iconic, culturally significant species. Here a nuanced understanding of local ecology, based in a historical connection to specific places, clearly reveals the importance of Indigenous interventions into the environment. Thus I decisively set aside the false claim of the pristine, untouched natural world to reveal the Gitxaała land- and marine-scapes as places created by Gitxaała and themselves creating the possibility of being Gitxaała.

Gitxaała choose to live on the most seaward edge of our territory. We are an ancient people who have lived in our laxyuup for millennia. Our history connects to our laxyuup, our home, back to the dawn of time.

We are also a contemporary modern people. We use cash, drive cars, and go to school. We understand our connections to the wider global world and know that this has changed us. However, as long as the ocean persists, Git lax m'oon will remain the people of the saltwater. We shall stand facing our future mindful of the importance of our past.

Notes

Introduction

The epigraph is from a meeting with Moody in 2008, recorded in Menzies and Rashleigh 2009.

1. My question of whether there is something epistemologically different that can be labeled an Indigenous methodology arises from my sense that the errors of past approaches lay in a lack of sensitivity and empathy to the people researchers were studying. That is, we were made into objects, translated into data, and our worlds were made laboratories for colonial practices. The difference between an Indigenous approach and a colonial one is, to me, a difference in political project, not epistemology.

1. Git lax m'oon

1. Joan Lovisek, expert opinion in *The Lax Kw'alaams Indian Band and Others v. The Attorney General of Canada and Her Majesty the Queen in Right of the Province of British Columbia*, prepared for James M. Mackenzie, Department of Justice, Vancouver, 2007.
2. These are unpublished consultant reports in the author's private files.
3. William Beynon, 1916, vol. 1, BF 419, box B29, p. 1, Canadian Museum of Civilization, Hull [hereafter CMC].
4. Each of these researchers published a great deal of material. I have chosen to cite their work only when I specifically engage with the content of their work. Here I name them as people of interest.
5. As with the mention of earlier ethnographers, these researchers are people of interest. When I engage their work directly, that work is cited.
6. William Beynon, "Ethnical and Geographical Study of the Tsimshian Nation," 1954, American Museum of Natural History, New York.

7. Wilson Duff's field notes can be found in the archives of the Museum of Anthropology at UBC.
8. George MacDonald, personal communication, June 17, 2009.
9. James McDonald, personal communication. (No date recorded. I spoke with him many times over the course of more than twenty years).

2. Smgigyet

1. I recorded these leaders in my field notes.
2. Adaawx is an oral record of "historical events of collective political, social, and economic significance, such as migration, territorial acquisition, natural disaster, epidemic, war, and significant shifts in political and economic power. . . . Adawx are formally acknowledged by the society as a whole and collectively represent the authorized history of the nation" (Marsden 2002, 102–3). Lach Klan is the contemporary village of Kitkatla, located on Dolphin Island.
3. Beynon's field notes can be found at the Canadian Museum of History, Columbia University, and the American Museum of Natural History.
4. Beynon notebook, 1916, BF 424, box B29, p. 7, CMC.
5. Andrew Martindale, personal communication, November 5, 2007.
6. We have conducted archaeological research at and near this village site and have C-14 dates showing occupation of this area dating back at least four thousand years. It is very likely, given the stratigraphy of these archaeological sites, that the flood event mentioned in the narrative preceded the C-14 dates that we have because the stratigraphy shows continuous human occupation, with no abandonment, over four millennia.
7. See Galois (2004, 2–4) for a brief biography of James Colnett. Colnett was born in Devon, England, in 1753. He "spent three and a half years under the tutelage of [James] Cook" (2). In 1786 he left the British Navy and "signed on with Richard Cadman Etches & Co as captain of the *Prince of Wales* and commander of a two-vessel commercial venture" (3).
8. While this location is near Tuwartz Inlet, Marsden (2002) is mistaken about the precise geographical location, which is at the southerly end of Pitt Island, just to the east behind Cherry Islets. The village is located on the Gitxaała reserve, Citeyats, where I have been involved in archaeological research in collaboration with other Gitxaała.
9. The Canadian state has attempted to regulate Indigenous food production through legislation that uses the criminal code to discipline and control Indigenous people. For example, harvesting fish by traditional means

outside of the state's regulatory process is a criminal act under the Fisheries Act. See Anderson (2007) for a discussion of diabetes and Gitxaała.

10. See also the narrative by Dorothy Brown (1992; Dunn 1969). Brown says Sabaan does not receive his name from the Europeans; rather he claims that they already know his name.

11. Galois (2004) notes that it is filed as B234, file 4 (war texts), CMC.

12. The full context and translation of He:l wiheld'm wildǝł nǝkłǝlstɔ'lt, "The offspring of beaver sits in many places," is in Beynon notebooks, 1916, vol. 6, BF 419–24, CMC.

13. Using carbon 14 dating, samples that our collaborative UBC-Gitxaała research team has collected from the areas near Ts'ibasaa's original home in Gitxaała territory date back at least four thousand years. We do not yet have any processed dates from the site of his first village, but the context is such as to suggest antiquity similar to those places that we do have dates from. C14 data in author's files and available upon request.

3. Laxyuup

1. Community meeting at the Highliner Inn, Prince Rupert, June 16, 2008.

2. Community research workshop, North West Community College, January 2008.

3. See also McIlwraith's Bella Coola Notes, 1922–24, 47, held in the Ethnology Division of the Canadian Museum of Civilization, Ottawa.

4. Federal Collection, Minutes of Decision, Correspondence and Sketches, P. O'Reilly, June 1882 to February 1885, file 29858, vol. 4 [Reg. B-64645], Federal Archives Canada, Vancouver.

5. William Beynon Manuscripts, undated, no. 100, Gitxaała Archives, Lach Klan.

6. Marius Barbeau Fonds, B.Mc21188(2), CMC.

7. Beynon writes that his "informant" was Joshua Tsibassa.

8. Joining our crew on this trip were Andrew Martindale, PhD (UBC associate professor of archaeology) and Kisha Supernant, PhD (University of Alberta assistant professor of archaeology).

9. See Miller (1981), for example, where he discusses the ways in which Klemtu—comprising at least two very different peoples—came into being around an industrial salmon cannery in the late 1800s.

4. Adaawx

1. Nathan Shaw was a hereditary leader interviewed numerous times by William Beynon in the early part of the twentieth century.

2. This is a reference to the new communities of Metlakatla (founded by

the missionary William Duncan in the late 1800s) and Port Simpson (founded by the Hudson's Bay Company in the early 1800s).

5. Sihoon

1. This date of five thousand years references the time when sea levels stabilized on the north coast of BC following the end of the ice age. Archaeologists working in adjoining areas to the west and north have, through modeling, found evidence of older human habitation both above and below current sea levels.
2. C14 data in author's files.
3. See Ames (2005, 365–82) for a list of fish and other faunal remains found in the Prince Rupert Harbor area. Matson and Coupland (1995) and Suttles (1990, 16–29) list a wide compendium of fish and other fauna that they suggest would have been used and may continue to be used by Indigenous peoples along the Northwest Coast.
4. A series of rock walls in Kitkatla Inlet may be more accurately understood as clam gardens or terraces rather than stone fish traps. I have had the opportunity to visit other locations within Gitxaała territory that may also be better understood as clam terracing rather than stone fish traps.
5. "The Purchase of Nauhulk" by James Lewis, recorded by William Beynon, n.d., narrative 70, Gitxaała Archives, Lach Klan.
6. William Beynon, "Tsimshian Geographical and Ethnical Material," notebook 6, p. 25, American Museum of Natural History, New York.
7. For example, there are a series of adaawx that document the alliances and conflicts involving Ts'ibasaa and other Ts'msyen smgigyet. For example, see the following, recorded by Beynon and archived in Gitxaała Archives, Lach Klan: Henry Watt (Nisnawhl, Kitkatla), "A Challenge Feast of Tsibasa," 1948–49; Matthew Johnson (Laraxnits, Gispaxloats), "Legaix Cremates Himself," 1926; James Lewis (Kaimtkwa, Kitkatla), "The Rise of Kitkatla over the Tsimshian," , 1947.
8. Here I list the key late twentieth-century linguists who worked with Tsimshianic languages. As I am not directly engaging with their publications; I only reference their names.
9. Margaret Anderson, personal communication, October 11, 1997. See also entries under *buy, gift, sell,* and *trade* in the Sm'algyax Dictionary, Ts'msyen Sm'algyax Authority, Prince Rupert, January 2001.
10. Sm'algyax Dictionary.
11. See Memorandum of Understanding between the Province of BC and the

Federal Government of Canada, November 9, 1912, GR 435, box 16, file 137, British Columbia Archives, Victoria.

12. Memorandum of Understanding.

6. Tsk̲ah, Xs'waanx

1. George Wood, March 3, 2000, affidavit in respect of *Kitkatla Band v. The Minister of Fisheries and Oceans*, Federal Court, docket T-284-00.
2. *Kitkatla Band v. The Minister of Fisheries and Oceans.*

7. Bilhaa

Reprinted by permission of Human Organization (vol. 69, no. 3).

1. Andrew Martindale, personal communication, February 15, 2007; Natalie Brewster, personal communication, November 2, 2007. My own archaeological research clearly and unambiguously documents an extensive and long-standing practice of bilhaa harvests (Menzies 2015).
2. This study surveys shellfish harvesting in the Northwest Coast ethnographic area with particular attention to the Tlingit.

8. Hoon

1. Sessional papers are reports and papers that have been tabled in the House of Commons (and sometimes the Senate) and deposited with the clerk. These papers include annual reports of government departments and boards and the estimates, public accounts, and reports of the royal commissions.
2. Sessional Papers 12, vol. 10, 1890.
3. Galois (2004) misidentifies, I think, the location of this event to a point a few miles to the south of Kxooyax. However, having visited both places many times and considering the information recorded by Colnett, the most plausible location is in fact Kxooyax.
4. P. O'Reilly, Minutes of Decision, Correspondence and Sketches, April 1889 to January 1892, file 29858, vol. 6 [Reg. B-64647], Federal Collection, Vancouver.
5. F. A. Devereux, field books, 1891–92, pp. 448–51, British Columbia Archives, Victoria.
6. Bare Bay is the common name used to refer to the bay into which Kxooyax Creek empties.
7. Indian Affairs, RG 10, vol. 3828, file 60,926 (reel C 10145), UBC Library, Vancouver.

8. Royal Commission on Indian Affairs for the Province of BC, Transcripts of Evidence, Questions Affecting the Fishing Rights, Interests and Privileges of Indians in British Columbia, Bella Coola Agency, pp. 1–33, British Columbia Archives, Victoria.

References

Agar, Michael H. 1996. *The Professional Stranger: An Informal Introduction to Ethnography*. 2nd ed. San Diego: Academic Press.

Ames, Kenneth M. 2005. *The North Coast Prehistory Project Excavations in the Prince Rupert Harbour, British Columbia: The Artifacts*. Oxford: British Archaeological Reports.

Ames, Kenneth M., and Herbert Maschner. 1999. *Peoples of the Northwest Coast: Their Archeology and Prehistory*. New York: Thames and Hudson.

Anderson, Margaret (Sequin), and Marjorie Halpin, eds. 2000. *Potlatch at Gitsegukla: William Beynon's 1945 Field Notebooks*. Vancouver: UBC Press.

Anderson, Robin. 2007. "Diabetes in Gitxaała: Colonization, Assimilation, and Economic Change." MA thesis, University of British Columbia, Vancouver.

Basso, Keith. 1996. *Wisdom Sits in Places: Landscape and Language among the Western Apache*. Albuquerque: University of New Mexico Press.

Benjamin, Walter. 1969. "The Storyteller: Reflections on the Works of Nikolai Leskov." In *Illuminations*, edited by Hannah Arendt, 83–109. New York: Schocken Books.

Berringer, Patricia. 1982. "Northwest Coast Traditional Salmon Fisheries Systems of Resource Utilization." MA thesis, University of British Columbia, Vancouver.

Blake, Michael. 2004. "Fraser Valley Trade and Prestige as Seen from Scowlitz." In *Complex Hunter-Gathers; Evolution and Organization of Prehistoric Communities of the Plateau of Northwestern North America*, edited by William C. Prentiss and Ian Kuijt, 103–12. Salt Lake City: University of Utah Press.

Boas, Franz. 1916. *Tsimshian Mythology*. Smithsonian Institution. Bureau of American Ethnology. Annual Report, 1909–10. Washington DC: Smithsonian Institution.

————. 1921. *Ethnology of the Kwakiutl: Based on Data Collected by George Hunt.* 35th Annual Report of the Bureau of American Ethnology (1913–14). In two parts. Washington DC: Government Printing Office.

Bolton, Richard. 2007. "Far West Point Site: Early Holocene Faunal Assemblage." Poster presentation at Department of Anthropology, UBC, Vancouver.

Boyd, Robert. 1999. *The Coming of the Spirit of Pestilence: Introduced Infectious Diseases and Population Decline among Northwest Coast Indians, 1774–1874.* Vancouver: UBC Press.

Brown, Dorothy. 1992. "Sabaan." In *Suwilaay'msga Na Ga'niiyatgm: Teachings of Our Grandfathers,* edited by Susan Marsden and Vonnie Hutchinson, 7–23. Prince Rupert, Canada: School District 52.

Butler, Caroline F. 2004. "Researching Traditional Ecological Knowledge for Multiple Uses." *Canadian Journal of Native Education* 28 (1–2): 33–48.

Campbell, Kenneth. 2005. *Persistence and Continuity: A History of the Tsimshian Nation.* Prince Rupert, Canada: School District 52.

Copes, Parcival. 1998. *Coping with the Coho Crisis: A Conservation-Minded, Stakeholder-Sensitive, and Community-Oriented Strategy.* Victoria: BC Ministry of Fisheries.

Coulthard, Glen. 2014. *Red Skin, White Masks: Rejecting the Colonial Politics of Recognition.* Minneapolis: University of Minnesota Press.

Coupland, Gary. 1985. "Prehistoric Culture Change at Kitselas Canyon." PhD dissertation, University of British Columbia, Vancouver.

Cove, John. 1987. *Shattered Images: Dialogues and Meditations on Tsimshian Narratives.* Carleton Library Series, no. 139. Ottawa: Carleton University Press.

Cove, John J., and George F. MacDonald, eds. 1987. *Tsimshian Narratives: Collected by Marius Barbeau and William Beynon.* Canadian Museum of Civilization Mercury Series, Directorate Paper 3. Vol. 1. Ottawa: Directorate, Canadian Museum of Civilization.

Dee, Henry Drummond, ed. 1945. *The Journal of John Work, January to October, 1835: Memoir No. X.* Victoria: Archives of British Columbia.

Dorsey, George A. 1897. "The Geography of the Tsimshian Indians." *American Antiquarian and Oriental Journal* 19(5): 276–82.

Drucker, Phillip. 1943. *Archeological Survey on the Northern Northwest Coast.* Washington DC: U.S. Government Printing Office.

Dunn, John A. 1969. "Old Migrations and New Dialects among the Coast Tsimshian." Paper presented at the North West Anthological Conference, Victoria.

————. 1976. "Tsimshian Internal Relations Reconsidered (Part 1)." Paper presented at the Northwest Studies Conference, Burnaby, BC.

Dwyer, Kevin. 1982. *Moroccan Dialogues: Anthropology in Question*. Baltimore: Johns Hopkins University Press.

Dyck, Noel. 1993. "'Telling It Like It Is': Some Dilemmas of Fourth World Ethnography and Advocacy." In *Anthropology, Public Policy, and Native Peoples in Canada*, edited by Noel Dyck and James Waldram, 192–212. Montreal: McGill-Queen's University Press.

Eldridge, Morley, and Alyssa Parker. 2007. Fairview Container Terminal Phase II Archaeological Overview Assessment, March 8. In author's possession.

Fanon, Frantz. 1963. *The Wretched of the Earth*. Preface by Jean-Paul Sartre. Translated by Constance Farrington. New York: Grove Press.

Galois, Robert, ed. 2004 *A Voyage to the North West Side of America: The Journals of James Colnett, 1786–89*. Vancouver: UBC Press.

Garibaldi, Ann, and Nancy J. Turner. 2004. "Cultural Keystone Species: Implications for Ecological Conservation and Restoration. *Ecology and Society* 9 (3): 1, http://www.ecologyandsociety.org/vol9/iss3/art1.

Garfield, Viola Edmundson. 1939. *Tsimshian Clan and Society*. University of Washington Publications in Anthropology, vol. 7, no. 3. Seattle: University of Washington.

Gislason, Gordon, et al. 1996. *Fishing for Answers: Coastal Communities and the BC Salmon Fishery: Final Report*. Victoria: Ministry of Agriculture, Fisheries, and Food.

Glavin, Terry. 1996. *Dead Reckoning: Confronting the Crisis in Pacific Fisheries*. Vancouver: Greystone Books.

Gluckman, Max. 1958. *Analysis of a Social Situation in Modern Zululand*. Manchester, UK: Manchester University Press.

Halpin, Marjorie. 1973. "The Tsimshian Crest System: A Study Based on Museum Specimens and the Marius Barbeau and William Beynon Fieldnotes." PhD dissertation, University of British Columbia, Vancouver.

————. 1984. "The Structure of Tsimshian Totemism." In *The Tsimshian and Their Neighbors of the North Pacific Coast*, edited by Jay Miller and Carol M. Eastman, 16–35. Seattle: University of Washington Press.

Halpin, Marjorie, and Margaret Seguin. 1990. "Tsimshian Peoples: Southern Tsimshian, Coast Timshian, Nishga, and Gitksan." In *Handbook of North American Indians*. Vol. 7: *Northwest Coast*, edited by Wayne Suttles, 267–84. Washington DC: Smithsonian Institution.

Harris, Cole. 2002. *Making Native Space*. Vancouver: UBC Press.

Harris, Douglas C. 2008. *Landing Native Fisheries: Indian Reserves and Fishing Rights in British Columbia.* Vancouver: UBC Press.

Ignas, Veronica, and Kenneth Campbell. 2009. "Traditional Ecological Knowledge and Climate Change." Curriculum Materials. Vancouver: Department of Anthropology, UBC.

Inglis, Gordon B., Douglas R. Hudson, Barbara K. Rigsby, and Bruce Rigsby. 1990. "Tsimshian of British Columbia Since 1990." In *Handbook of North American Indians.* Vol. 7: *Northwest Coast,* edited by Wayne Suttles, 285–93. Washington DC: Smithsonian Institution.

Inglis, Richard I. 2011. "History of the Establishment Kitkatla (Gitxaała) Indian Reserves." Unpublished report.

Jones, Russ, N. A. Sloan, and Bart DeFreitas. 2004. "Prospects for Northern Abalone (*Haliotis Kamtschatkana*) Recovery in Haida Gwaii through Community Stewardship." In *Making Ecosystem Based Management Work: Connecting Managers and Researchers. Proceedings of the Fifth International Conference on Science and Management of Protected Areas, 11–16, May 2003,* edited by N. W. P. Munro, P. Dearden, T. B. Herman, K. Beazley, and S. Bondrup-Nielsen. CD-ROM. Wolfville, Nova Scotia: SAMPAA.

Kelly, R. L., and M. Prasciunas. 2007. "Did the Ancestors of Native Americans Cause Animal Extinctions in Late Pleistocene North America?" In *Native Americans and the Environment: Perspectives on the Ecological Indian,* edited by M. E. Harkin and D. R. Lewis, 95–122. Lincoln: University of Nebraska Press.

Kew, Michael. 1989. "Salmon Availability, Technology and Cultural Adaptations on the Fraser River." In *A Complex Culture of the British Columbia Plateau: Traditional Stl'atl'imx Resource Use,* edited by Bryan Hayden, 177–221. Vancouver: UBC Press.

Knight, Rolf. 1996. *Indians at Work: An Informal History of Native Labour in British Columbia, 1848–1930.* Vancouver: New Star Books.

Kobrinsky, Vernon. 1975. "Dynamics of the Fort Rupert Class Struggle: Fighting with Property Vertically Revisited." In *Papers in Honor of Harry Hawthorn,* edited by V. Serl and H. Taylor, 32–59. Bellingham: Western Washington State College.

Langdon, Stephen. 2006. "Tidal Pulse Fishing: Selective Traditional Tlingit Salmon Fishing Techniques on the West Coast of the Prince of Wales Archipelago." In *Traditional Ecological Knowledge and Natural Resource Management,* edited by Charles R. Menzies, 21–46. Lincoln: University of Nebraska Press.

Lutz, John S. 2008. *Makúk: A New History of Aboriginal-White Relations*. Vancouver: UBC Press.

MacDonald, George F., and John J. Cove, eds. 1987. *Tsimshian Narratives: Collected by Marius Barbeau and William Beynon*. Canadian Museum of Civilization Mercury Series, Directorate Paper 3, vol. 2. Ottawa: Directorate, Canadian Museum of Civilization.

MacDonald, Joanne. 1990. "From Ceremonial Object to Curio: Object Transformation at Port Simpson and Merlakatla, British Columbia in the Nineteenth Century." *Canadian Journal of Native Studies* 10 (2): 193–217.

———. 2015. "In the Blink of an Eye: Collecting the Tsimshian Stone Masks." In *Of One Heart: Gitxaała and Our Neighbours*, edited by Charles R. Menzies. Vancouver: New Proposals.

Mackie, Quentin, Daryl W. Fedje, Duncan McLaren, Nicole Smith, and Iain McKechnie. 2011. "Early Environments and Archaeology of Coastal British Columbia." In *Trekking the Shore: Changing Coastlines and the Antiquity of Coastal Settlement*, edited by N. F. Bicho, J. A. Haws, and L. G. Davis, 51–103. Interdisciplinary Contributions to Archaeology. New York: Springer.

Marsden, Susan. 2002. "Adawx, Spanaxnox, and the Geopolitics of the Tsimshian." *B.C. Studies* 135: 101–35.

Marsden, Susan, and Robert Galois. 1995. "The Tsimshian, the Hudson's Bay Company, and the Geopolitics of the Northwest Coast Fur Trade, 1787–1840." *Canadian Geographer/Le Géographe canadien* 39 (2): 169–83.

Marsden, Susan, and Vonnie Hutchinson, eds. 1992. *Suwilaay'msga Na Ga'niiyatgm: Teachings of Our Grandfathers*. Prince Rupert, Canada: School District 52.

Martindale, Andrew, Bryn Letham, Duncan McLaren, David Archer, Meghan Burchell, and Bernd R. Schone. 2009. "Mapping of Subsurface Shell Midden Components through Percussion Coring: Examples from the Dundas Islands." *Journal of Archaeological Science* 36 (9): 1565–75.

Matson, R. G., and Gary Coupland. 1995. *The Prehistory of the Northwest Coast*. San Diego: Academic Press.

McDonald, James A. 1984. "Images of the Nineteenth-Century Economy of the Tsimshian." In *The Tsimshian: Images of the Past, Views for the Present*, edited by Margaret Sequin, 40–54. Vancouver: UBC Press.

———. 1985. "Trying to Make a Life: The Historical Political Economy of Kitsumkalum." PhD dissertation, University of British Columbia, Vancouver.

———. 1990. "Bleeding Day and Night: The Construction of the Grand Trunk Pacific Railway across Tsimshian Reserve Lands." *Canadian Journal of Native Studies* 10 (1): 33–69.

———. 1991. "The Marginalization of the Tsimshian." In *Cultural Ecology: The Seasonal Cycle. Native Peoples, Native Lands: Canadian Indians, Inuit and Metis*, edited by Bruce Alden Cox, 109–216. Ottawa: Carleton University Press.

———. 1994. "Social Change and the Creation of Underdevelopment: A Northwest Coast Case." *American Ethnologist* 21 (1): 152–75.

McIlwraith, T. F. 1948. *The Bella Coola Indians*. 2 vols. Toronto: University of Toronto Press.

McKechnie, Iain, Dana Lepofsky, Madonna L. Moss, Virginia L. Butler, Trevor J. Orchard, Gary Coupland, Fredrick Foster, Megan Caldwell, and Ken Lertzman. 2014. "Archaeological Data Provide Alternative Hypotheses on Pacific Herring (*Clupea pallasii*) Distribution, Abundance, and Variability." *Proceedings of the National Academy of Sciences, USA* 111 (9): E807–E816.

McLaren, Duncan, Andrew Martindale, Daryl W. Fedje, and Quentin Mackie. 2011. "Relict Shorelines and Shell Middens of the Dundas Island Archipelago." *Canadian Journal of Archaeology* 35 (2): 86–116.

Menzies, Charles R. 1993. "All That Holds Us Together: Kinship and Resource Pooling in a Fishing Co-operative." *MAST: Maritime Anthropological Studies* 6 (1–2): 157–79.

———. 1994. "Stories from Home: First Nations, Land Claims, and Euro-Canadians." *American Ethnologist* 21 (4): 776–91.

———. 1996. "Indian or White? Racial Identities in the British Columbian Fishery." In *Anthropology for a Small Planet*, edited by Anthony Marcus, 110–23. St. James NY: Brandywine Press.

———. 2004. "Putting Words into Action: Negotiating Collaborative Research in Gitxaała." *Canadian Journal of Native Education* 28 (1–2): 15–32.

———. 2006. "Ecological Knowledge, Subsistence, and Livelihood Practices: The Case of the Pine Mushroom Harvest in Northwestern British Columbia." In *Traditional Ecological Knowledge and Natural Resource Management*, edited by Charles R. Menzies, 87–104. Lincoln: University of Nebraska Press.

———. 2010. "Dm sibilhaa'nm da laxyuubm Gitxaała: Picking Abalone in Gitxaała Territory." *Human Organization* 69 (3): 213–20.

———. 2011. "Butterflies, Anthropologies, and Ethnographic Field Schools: A Reply to Wallace and Hyatt." *Collaborative Anthropologies* 4: 260–66.

———. 2012. "The Disturbed Environment: The Indigenous Cultivation of Salmon." In *Keystone Nations: Indigenous Peoples and Salmon across the North Pacific*, edited by Benedict J. Colombi and James F. Brooks, 161–82. Santa Fe NM: School for Advanced Research.

———. 2015. "Revisiting 'Dm Sibilhaa'nm Da Laxyuubm Gitxaała (Picking Abalone in Gitxaała Territory)': Vindication, Appropriation, and Archaeology." *BC Studies*, no. 187 (Autumn): 129–55.

Menzies, Charles R., and Caroline F. Butler. 2001. "Working in the Woods: Tsimshian Resource Workers and the Forest Industry of BC." *American Indian Quarterly* 25 (3): 409–30.

Menzies, Charles R., and Caroline F. Butler. 2007. "Returning to Selective Fishing through Indigenous Knowledge: The Example of K'moda Gitxaała Territory." *American Indian Quarterly* 31 (3): 441–62.

Menzies, Charles R., and Caroline F. Butler. 2008. "The Indigenous Foundation of the Resource Economy of BC's North Coast." *Labour/Le Travail* 61 (Spring): 131–49.

Menzies, Charles R., and Caroline F. Butler. 2011. "Collaborative Service Learning and Anthropology with Gitxaała Nation. With Reflections by Solen Roth, Natalie J. K. Baloy, Robin Anderson, Jennifer Wolowic, and Oralia Gómez-Ramírez and Concluding Comments by Nees Ma'Outa (Clifford White)." *Collaborative Anthropologies* 4:169–242.

Menzies, Charles R., and Jennifer Rashleigh, directors. 2009. *Bax Laanks— Pulling Together: A Story of Gitxaała Nation*. Vancouver: UBC Ethnographic Film Unit.

Miller, Jay. 1981. "Moieties and Cultural America: Manipulation of Knowledge in a Pacific Northwest Coast Native Community [Corrected title: Moieties and Cultural Amnesia: Manipulation of Knowledge in a Pacific Northwest Coast Native Community]." *Arctic Anthropology* 18 (1): 23–32.

———. 1984. "Feasting with the Southern Tsimshian." In *The Tsimshian: Images of the Past, Views for the Present*, edited by Margaret Sequin, 27–39. Vancouver: UBC Press.

———. 1997. *Tsimshian Culture: A Light through the Ages*. Lincoln: University of Nebraska Press.

Mitchell, Donald. 1981. "Sebassa's Men." In *The World Is as Sharp as a Knife: An Anthology in Honour of Wilson Duff*, edited by Donald N. Abbott, 79–86. Victoria: British Columbia Provincial Museum.

Mitchell, Donald, and Leland Donald. 2001. "Sharing Resources on the North Pacific Coast of North America: The Case of the Eulachon Fishery." *Anthropologica* 43 (1): 19–35.

Moss, Madonna L. 1993. "Shellfish, Gender, and Status on the Northwest Coast: Reconciling Archeological, Ethnographic, and Ethnohistorical Records of the Tlingit." *American Anthropologist*, n.s., 95 (3): 631–52.

Muszynski, Alicj. 1996. *Cheap Wage Labour: Race and Gender in the Fisheries of British Columbia*. Montreal: McGill-Queen's University Press.

Newell, Dianne. 1993. *Tangled Webs of History: Indians and the Law in Canada's Pacific Coast Fisheries*. Toronto: University of Toronto Press.

———. 1999. "'Overlapping Territories and Entwined Cultures': A Voyage into the Northern BC Spawn-on-Kelp Fishery." In *Fishing Places, Fishing People: Traditions and Issues in Canadian Small-Scale Fisheries*, edited by Rosemary Ormmer and Dianne Newell, 121–44. Toronto: University of Toronto Press.

Pritchard, John C. 1977. "Economic Development and the Disintegration of Traditional Culture among the Haisla." PhD dissertation, University of British Columbia, Vancouver.

Roe, Michael, ed. 1967. *The Journal and Letters of Captain Charles Bishop on the North-West Coast of America, in the Pacific and in New South Wales, 1794–1799*. Cambridge, UK: Cambridge University Press.

Roth, Christopher F. 2008. *Becoming Tsimshian: The Social Life of Names*. Seattle: University of Washington Press.

Seguin (Anderson), Margaret. 1984. "Lest There Be No Salmon." In *The Tsimshian: Images of the Past, Views for the Present*, edited by Margaret Sequin, 110–33. Vancouver: UBC Press.

Sewid, James, and James Spradley. 1969. *Guests Never Leave Hungry: The Autobiography of James Sewid, a Kwakiutl Indian*. New Haven CT: Yale University Press.

Simonsen, Bjorn O. 1973. *Archaeological Investigations in the Hecate Strait–Milbanke Sound Area of British Columbia*. Ottawa: National Museum of Man.

Smethurst, Naomi. 2014. "Inscribed on the Landscape: Stories of Stone Traps and Fishing in Laxyuup Gitxaała." MA thesis, University of British Columbia, Vancouver.

Smith, Linda Tuhiwai. 1999. *Decolonizing Methodologies: Research and Indigenous Peoples*. New York: Zed Books.

Stewart, Hillary. 1977. *Indian Fishing: Early Methods on the Northwest Coast*. Seattle: University of Washington Press.

Suttles, Wayne. 1987. *Coast Salish Essays*. Seattle: University of Washington Press.

———. 1990. "Environment." In *Handbook of North American Indians*. Vol. 7: *Northwest Coast*, edited by Wayne Suttles, 16–29. Washington DC: Smithsonian Institution.

Tilley, Christopher. 2010. *Interpreting Landscapes*. Walnut Creek CA: Left Coast Press.

Tolmie, W. Fraser. 1963. *Physician and Fur Trader: The Journals of William Fraser Tolmie*. Vancouver: Mitchell Press.

Turner, Nancy J., and Helen Clifton. 2006. "The Forest and the Seaweed." In *Traditional Ecological Knowledge and Natural Resource Management*, edited by Charles R. Menzies, 65–86. Lincoln: University of Nebraska Press.

Wagner, Henry R., and W. A. Newcombe, eds. 1938. "The Journal of Don Jacinto Caamano." Translated by Harold Grenfell. *British Columbia Historical Quarterly*, July–October: 189–301.

Wigen, Becky. 2012. "Vertebrate Fauna from Gitxaała Augers." Unpublished report. Victoria: Pacific Identifications.

Winter, Barbara J. 1984. "William Beynon and the Anthropologists." *Canadian Journal of Native Studies* 2: 279–92.

Wolf, Eric R. 1999. *Envisioning Power: Ideologies of Dominance and Crisis*. Berkeley: University of California Press.

Index

Dunn, John, 15–17, 25
Dwyer, Kevin, 6
Dyck, Noel, 25

"Ecological Indian" myth, 131–32
ecological problems, 8–9, 117–18, 148
economy, contemporary, 24–25;
    aboriginal people excluded from,
    100, 102–5, 117–18; traditional
    model integrated with, 99–100,
    105, 121
Estevan Group, 49, 64
"Ethnical and Geographical Study of
    the Tsimshian Nation" (Beynon),
    23, 24, 30–31
Europeans: not respecting Gitxaała
    law, 33, 96; violence committed
    by, 34
extractive resource industries, 2,
    42–45; double standard in
    monitoring of, 128–29; fishing and,
    97–98, 101–3, 114, 117–18, 127–29;
    Gitxaała as labor for, 98, 136;
    indigenous responses to, 18, 43–45

feasts, 32; seaweed served at, 93;
    silence at, 72–73; telling history
    at, 72–73
Fisheries Act, 156n9Chap2
fishing, 87–105, 107–18; aboriginal
    people denied rights to, 99, 101–2,
    104–5, 117–18, 119–21; archeologi-
    cal evidence of, 90, 91, 95–96,
    109–11; in cannery-owned boats,
    104; capitalism changing, 42–44,
    50, 97–105; contemporary,
    97–105; gear, 134, 146–47; and
    Gitxaała cultural values, 8–9,
    87–90, 91, 120–21; at K'moda,

134–38, 147; licenses, 97, 99, 103,
    104–5, 139–40; nontarget species,
    147–48; in oral histories, 88–90;
    politics of, 5–6, 8, 49–50, 152;
    race and, 102–3; and respect,
    87–90; seasonal, 33, 108, 111, 134;
    severed from processing, 144;
    stock management in, 90, 121–22,
    133–34, 148; sustainably, 98,
    124–30, 132–35, 152; techniques,
    90–92, 108–9, 116–17, 121–22,
    124–27, 137; terminology for, 95;
    and title holders of fisheries,
    52–53, 75, 98, 142–43, 146, 147;
    for trade, 93–96, 99–100, 102;
    visiting sites of, 64, 82–84;
    women and children and, 99
fish traps, 83–84, 90, 108, 124,
    131–32; design of, 137–38, 141; for
    different types of salmon, 143;
    drag seines replacing, 143–44; at
    Kxooyax, 138–41, 143, 147, 159n3;
    selectivity of, 148
the flood/deluge, 31, 48, 156n6
food harvesting, 85; of abalone,
    124–30; archeological research
    into, 60, 66, 90–91, 96, 108–11,
    123–24; criminalization of
    aboriginal methods of, 37, 44, 50,
    133, 156n9Chap2; drying, 109, 125,
    145; foraging, 137; hunting,
    136–37; and population decline,
    113–14, 137, 144; yearly cycle of,
    145. See also fishing
foodways, changing, 111–15, 126,
    127–28

Galois, Robert, 40, 157n11, 159n3
Gamble, Edward, 2, 135, 137, 147

legal battles (*continued*)
    over fishing rights, 19; over
    laxyuup (territory), 50–51, 75–82
Lewis, James, 94, 144
Lewis, Russell, 126–27, 128
Lewis, Samuel, 56, 70, 81
Lewis, Samuel Wise, 145
Lewis, William, 144
light and luminosity, 123
lik'agyet (councilors), 27
Lovisek, Joan, 19

MacDonald, George, 19, 22, 25, 96, 124
MacDonald, Joanne, 19, 25
malsk (telling), 71–72; as right to tell
    stories, 71
marriage, 35
Marsden, Susan, 15, 17–18, 22,
    156n8Chap2
Martindale, Andrew, 19, 22, 123,
    157n8; on the flood, 31
Maschner, Herbert, 96
matrilineality, 34, 35
Matson, R. G., 96, 158n3
McCauley, George, 40
McDonald, James, 18, 22, 24, 25, 101
McIlwraith, T. F., 49
McKenna-McBride Commission, 100
Menzies, Basso, 82, 83, 107, 108, 115,
    135
Menzies, Charles R.: archeological
    work of, 38–39, 91, 96, 109–10,
    124, 156n6, 157n13; family of, 2–3,
    4, 82, 83–84, 107–8, 131–32, 135;
    fishing, 107, 116–17, 132; helping
    with legal issues, 79; K'moda and,
    66, 82–84, 135–38; Kxooyax
    visited by, 140–41; Lach Klan
    visited by, 3–4; in Prince Rupert,

5–6; on sustainable fishing, 129,
    132; watershed restoration work
    of, 132; working collaboratively
    with Band Council, 4–5
Menzies, Shirley Marie, 2
Menzies, Tristan, 79
methodology, 1–2, 4–9; collaborative,
    4–5; decolonizing, 6–7; Indige-
    nous, 6–7, 155n1Intro; of soil
    samples, 109–11; for translation, 75
Metlakatla, 14, 17, 53, 76, 157n2Chap4
migration, seasonal, 49, 99
Miller, Jay, 17, 18, 22; on cultural
    importance of light, 123; on
    fishing, 88–89, 157n9; *Tsimshian
    Culture*, 16
missionary communities, 15, 53, 75
Mitchell, Donald, 49
Moody, Elmer, 1, 11; on governance, 28
Moody, Janet, 76–77, 125, 127–28
Moore Island, 64
Morrison, M. K., 139–40
Moss, Madonna, 123
Muszynski, Alicja, 99
"The Myth of the Adventures of
    Gom'asnext" (Beynon), 53

names: changing, 39–40; geography
    and, 66, 75–82, 151–52; given by
    anthropologists, 13–14, 15–16, 17–18,
    19–20; given by traders, 33, 41,
    157n10; hereditary, 27, 29–30, 35,
    38; language of, 21; legal meanings
    of, 15; and relationality, 151–52; and
    self-identification, 15, 18
Naming the Harbour (film), 79
natural world, aboriginal impact on,
    131–32, 141, 148–49, 152
naxnox (supernatural being), 71–72

Nees Ma'Outa, 34
nettle twine nets, 144
Newell, Dianne, 25
Nisga'a, 13–14, 20; governance, 29
Nisga'a language, 15
Northern Coast-Tsimshian people, 17–18, 50

"official ethnography," 25
oil: herring, 109; seal, 92
Oka Crisis, 5
oral history. See *adaawx* (oral record); history
O'Reilly, Peter, 44, 48; reserves established by, 51–53, 64, 101, 139

phratries (clans), 54
Pitt Island, 31, 49, 56–57, 61, 62, 156n8Chap2
place, connection to. See *laxyuup* (territory)
place-names workshop, 75–79, 84
population decline, 37–39, 59, 112–14; economic opportunities follow- ing, 114; food harvesting affected by, 113–14, 137, 144
Port Essington BC, 97
Port Simpson, 14, 17, 36, 53
Prince, Paul, 22
Prince Rupert BC, 97
Prince Rupert Fishermen's Co- operative, 104
Prince Rupert Harbor: archeological findings at, 158n3; name of, 79–82, 84; ownership of, 75–79
Pritchard, John, 24, 42

railroads, 97
Rashleigh, Jen, 79

reciprocity, 87–88, 132–33
regalia, 32, 122–23
reserves: establishment of, 48, 51–53; fishing on, 101, 139; *laxyuup* (territory) and, 50–53; smallness of, in BC, 100
Robinson, Rita, 77–78
Roth, Christopher, 22

Sabaan, 39–40, 91, 142, 157n10
sagyook (trade), 95
salmon, 8, 9, 131–49; canning industry, 97–100, 104, 114, 135–36; decline of, 90, 133, 147–48; and hereditary fisheries, 52–53, 66, 91, 97, 147; management, 44, 133–35, 147–48, 152; sustainable harvest of, 98, 133–35, 137–41; types of, 53, 143, 147–48
saltwater, 1, 11, 64, 152–53
seals: hunting, 64, 114; oil from, 92
sea otters, 114
seaweed harvesting, 92–93
Seax: Bishop meeting, 32–33; Colnett meeting, 31–32, 33; fishing rights and, 44, 139–40; reserve territory and, 52
Sebassah, Paul, 51–52, 99
"Sebassa" Indians, 33
Seguin, Margaret. See Anderson, Margaret Seguin
Sessional Papers, 136, 159n1Chap8
Shaw, Agnes, 125, 144–46
Shaw, Joseph, 77
Shaw, Nathan, 80, 157n1Chap4
shellfish, 92. See also abalone
sigyidm hana'a (matriarchs), 27
sihoon (catching fish), 87
silence, 72–73

Simonsen, Bjorn, 96
Skeena River, 43–44
Skog, Violet, 125
Sky Brothers, 31
sm'algyax (Tsimshianic language), 21, 75, 158n9
smallpox, 113
smgigyet (real people), 27–29, 35; capitalism and, 43–45
Smith, Linda Tuhiwai: *Decolonizing Methodologies*, 7
sm'ooygit (ranking hereditary leader), 27, 35; paying respect to, 36–37
social class, 34–35, 122–23
social landscape, 59–66
soil, anthropogenic, 61, 110–11
Southern Tsimshian language, 15–16
Spencer, Jeffrey, 126, 127
Spencer, Job, 56
Spencer, Marc, 89–90
Spencer, Richard, 77–78, 80, 81; on governance, 28–29
stone traps. *See* fish traps
streamscaping, 132–33, 138–41. *See also* fish traps
"subsistence," 93–94, 101–2, 136
Supernant, Kisha, 157n8
Sussman, Amelia, 22, 23
Suttles, Wayne, 158n3
syt güülum goot (being of one heart), 122, 127

Tait, John, 88
Temlax'am, 35–36
terraces, 61
territory. See *laxyuup* (territory)
Tilley, Christopher, 60
timber: compensation for, 101; trade in, restricted, 100–101

trade: in fish, 93–96, 99–100, 102; linguistic data for, 95; networks, 94, 100; in roe, 114, 115
Ts'ibasaa, 33, 35, 157n13; changing name to He:l, 39, 40–42; houses of, 65–66; reserves and, 44, 51, 64
Tsibassa, Joshua, 40–41, 53, 56; granting approval for telling stories, 70–71; as source for Beynon, 40, 41, 157n7
Tsimshian Clan and Society (Garfield), 22
Tsimshian Culture (Miller), 16
Tsimshianic languages, 15–17
Tsimshianic peoples, 13–14, 15; Coast and Southern, 18, 19, 20; disputed origins of, 19; postcontact movements of, 17, 24; tripartite model of, 17–18
tskah (herring), 8, 91, 107–18, 152
Ts'msyen, 15, 19, 20, 43–44; Gitxaała distinguishing themselves from, 48
Turner, Nancy, 93
Txemsum, 88

values, fishing and, 8–9, 87–90, 91, 120–21
villages, 36, 55, 56–58, 60–66; dating, 30–31, 59, 61, 62, 66, 84; described by Bishop, 64–65

'wa'at (sell), 95
walp (house group), 34–35, 55; resource-gathering governed by, 35, 148; territories of, 56–58
wars with Haida, 80–81
white settlers, 102–3

CPSIA information can be obtained
at www.ICGtesting.com
Printed in the USA
LVOW12*1658070716

495493LV00004B/31/P

9 780803 288089